Mustard-Seed Churches

Mustard-Seed Churches

Ministries in Small Churches

■

Robert B. Coote
Editor

FORTRESS PRESS ■ MINNEAPOLIS

MUSTARD-SEED CHURCHES
Ministries in Small Churches

Cover design: Ned Skubic
Cover photo: Pamela Harper
Internal design: Peregrine Publications

Library of Congress Cataloging-in-Publication Data
Mustard-seed churches : ministries in the small churches / Robert B.
    Coote, editor.
        p.   cm.
    Includes bibliographical references.
    ISBN 0-8006-2408-4 (alk. paper)
    1. Small churches—United States.   2. Rural churches—United
States.   3. Pastoral theology.   I. Coote, Robert B., 1944-
BV637.8.M87   1990
253'.0973—dc20   90-30406
                                                                        CIP

The paper used in this publication meets the minimum requirements of American National Standard for Information Sciences—Permanence of Paper for Printed Library Materials, ANSI Z329.48-1984.   ∞™

Manufactured in the U.S.A.   AF 1-2408

94   93   92   91   90   1   2   3   4   5   6   7   8   9   10

Contents

Contributors

(Churches at Time of Writing)

John L. Anderson
   Springwater Presbyterian Church
   Estacada, Oregon

James Ayers
   First Presbyterian Church
   Kingman, Kansas

Benjamin E. Blumel
   Carrollton United Presbyterian Church
   Carrollton, Ohio

James Crislip
   Community Presbyterian Church
   Moro, Oregon

Thomas O. Elson
   First Presbyterian Church
   Lindsay, California

Susan M. Fleenor
   Heritage Presbyterian Church
   Benicia, California

Douglas J. Hale
   United Methodist Churches
   Sutherlin and Wilbur, Oregon

Rebecca Hazen
   Eagle Creek Presbyterian Church
   Eagle Creek, Oregon

Joanne D. Hines
   Kelseyville Presbyterian Church
   Kelseyville, California

Ellsworth E. Jackson
    Marksboro Presbyterian Church
    Marksboro, New Jersey

Wayne H. Keller
    Trinity United Presbyterian Church
    Sedro Woolley, Washington

Dorothy Price Knudson
    St. John's Chapel by the Sea
    Pacific Beach, Washington

Philip A. Nesset
    Church of the Mountains
    Hoopa, California

Jane Newstead
    First Presbyterian Church
    Odebolt, Iowa

David R. Ord
    Trinity Presbyterian Church
    Jonesville, Louisiana

Sandra L. Peirce
    El Dorado County Federated Church
    Placerville, California

Julio A. Ramirez
    Iglesia Presbiteriana Hispana
    Oakland, California

Chandler Stokes
    Community Presbyterian Church
    Garberville, California
        and
    Leggett Presbyterian Church
    Leggett, California

■ Introduction ■

Robert B. Coote

THE KINGDOM OF GOD, we are told, is like a grain of mustard seed. The smallest of seeds, it grows into the largest of herbs, and puts out large branches, so that birds can nest in its shade.

A seed like that is every small church minister's dream. The smallest becomes the largest—just what to expect in God's kingdom. Prosperity and church growth in the small church. Most people don't expect it, but in the Bible the unexpected happens all the time.

Of course with Jesus' parables there is often more than meets the eye. In Mark's version of the parable of the mustard seed, the earliest version in the Gospels, the seed becomes the largest of the *lachana*, "herbs" or "vegetables." The Revised Standard Version is even stretching things by calling it a "shrub." Maybe a *little* shrub. The central stem of the mustard plant is known occasionally to grow as high as a person, but usually if the plant gets to be three or four feet high, it has reached its limit. Most of its leaves grow near the ground. So what is the significance of a mustard plant? For Mark, the contrast between the tiny seed and the sizable herb was enough: smallest seed, large enough plant. If he had wanted to talk about sheer size and abundance, he might have chosen instead the august oak or mighty cedar.

Matthew saw a possibility in a scriptural allusion (apparent also to Mark) and decided to enlarge on Mark's version. "When the mustard seed is grown," says Jesus in Matthew, "it becomes the greatest of herbs, *and becomes a tree*." Now there is a miracle. The kingdom is like a mustard tree—hitherto unheard of— large enough for the birds to nest in its branches, not just in

1

its shade. Smallest seed, largest plant, and miraculous—like, say, a "broccoli tree." Luke left out the herbal stage altogether: "It grew and became a tree." Matthew and Luke augmented the idyll. For them the birds represent gentile Christians, a worthy motif. Sometimes theirs is the version to preach from.

But size is only one vector in the parable. In his allusion to a tree, Mark was thinking of a second vector. Mark was a scribe. He knew the phrase "the birds of the air can make nests in its shade" would remind people who knew the Scriptures of a prophecy in Ezekiel. This is what Matthew noticed. "I will take a sprig from the lofty top of the cedar," says the Lord in Ezekiel, "and I will plant it on a high mountain. On the mountain height of Israel will I plant it, so that it may bring forth branches and bear fruit, and become a noble cedar. Every kind of bird will dwell beneath it, and in the shadow of its branches they shall dwell. And all the trees of the field shall know that I the Lord bring low the high tree, and make high the low tree, wither the green tree, and make the withered tree flourish" (Ezek. 17:22-24).

In Mark, mustard represented the small made great, the low made high, and the dry made green. But then there is the next question. For Mark, what represented the corresponding great made small, high made low, and green made withered? For Mark, the great, high, and "green" were the large and lofty temple, conceived as the leafy fig tree, high on Zion, fruitless and hence deserving of the withering curse (Mark 11:11-23; based on Jer. 7:1-11; 8:13). In other words, in Mark the mustard stands for the contrast between two opposing institutions, the community of the faithful anticipating the kingdom of God, and the temple as the largest church in the society. In Mark, the mustard does not just grow. It replaces the cursed fig.

We need not press the analogy between temple and large church, nor the indelicate contrast between large church and small church, to recognize that the parable's second vector requires some contrast or opposition. This is a less benign approach to growth. Not everything can grow at once. It is a zero-sum game: for one thing to grow, something else has to shrink. The growth of the kingdom portends the withering of some opposing institution—which eventually requires identification.

In Ezekiel that institution was the Babylonian state, the political and economic giant of the day. This identification is corroborated by a second scriptural allusion made by the parable, this time to a story in Daniel based on Ezekiel's prophecy. In this story, the tree itself symbolizes the opposing institution. Nebuchadnezzar, the king of Babylon, sees the tree in a dream. "Its height was great. It grew and became strong, and its top reached to the heavens. Its leaves were fair and its fruit abundant, and in it was food for all. The beasts of the field found shade under it, and the birds of the air dwelt in its branches" (Dan. 4:10-12). Except for the allusion to the Tower of Babel or Babylon ("its top reached to the heavens"), we might think we were dealing with simply a peaceable idyll. What could be wrong with this scene?

The dream goes on. A holy one came down from heaven and cried out, "Hew down the tree! Cut off its branches, strip off its leaves, and scatter its fruit! Get the beasts out from under it and the birds out of its branches!" Daniel is compelled to advise the king of the biggest of the big powers of his day, "The tree is you, O king, who have grown and become strong."

No wonder Mark said nothing explicit about the mustard becoming a tree. A plant the size of mustard is fine. If, however, it keeps growing bigger and stronger, God might have to cut it down—even when it provides "food for all." In Mark's view, the temple and Rome, the biggest church and the Babylon of his day, and the culture of largeness they promote, conspired to keep most people from eating enough, and many from eating at all. They needed cutting down. The growth of God's kingdom suggested by the mustard seed portends the fall of the great church (temple) symbolized by the fig tree.

The little mustard plant thus leaves a question mark to be faced by the larger plants. Such irony typifies Mark. Children invalidate adults and their quest for greatness. Blind people invalidate the view of sighted people. Women, foreigners, Roman soldiers—all the lesser and despised people in the world of Palestine have more truth to say than the supposedly greater

3

people. Through no particular effort of their own, just by being who they are, the small stand in judgment of the large.

Mark may also have recognized a third vector. This was the meaning Jesus himself had in mind, which was quite different from the first two. Jesus was talking mainly to rural working folk who didn't read and who didn't go to the equivalent of church. They weren't much interested in abstract comparisons and allusions to Scripture. They were interested in how to grow food, and they knew all about mustard.

Mustard was a weed and a menace. The bigger the weed, the more the seed, the more the weeds, the more the grief. Up to four thousand seeds per plant, an average of twenty thousand seeds per ounce of seed. Mustard was one of the farmer's worst enemies. Once it took hold, it was extremely difficult to eradicate. Mustard was sown, if at all, in uncultivated fields, not Matthew's arable land or Luke's garden. It was hardly meant to "fall into good soil"—that was a different parable.

And who needs birds? Birds "come and devour it." Yet the kingdom, Jesus says, is like a giant mustard plant broadcasting a multitude of seed, a magnet to winged thieves who, once settled in, eat up the sower's good seed in the field as well. The mustard was the bane of the sower, the farmer's nightmare. Better the smallest seed should stay that way. (See Douglas E. Oakman, *Jesus and the Economic Questions of His Day*, Lewiston: Edwin Mellen Press, 1986, 123-28.)

What's going on? What has happened to the liberating gospel of the last becoming first, the smallest the largest? What was Jesus thinking of?

Jesus was in some ways more radical than Mark. Jesus knew that mustard was bad for the fields of grain. A large mustard plant and the birds it attracted could ruin a field. It would undermine the entire system of production, all parts of which were caught up in the corruption of the Roman and temple cult of largeness. Rome and the temple promoted intensification of production and the transformation of most of the working population of Palestine from landholders to wage laborers. Jesus' parable points to a profound disruption of the entire current order. That's what the kingdom of God as a little seed does.

Do small churches possibly bear such meaning in our context? That would be saying far more than what this book is about. The point of this collection of reflections is not to idealize or romanticize the small church. Quite the contrary. What these little essays do is to look candidly at ministry in the small church as it really is, with its defects as well as its graces.

Small churches, while as numerous as mustard seeds, are not usually thought of as the locus of prophetic ministry. Nevertheless, if we take a hint from the parable of the mustard seed, we might do well to wonder whether we all have something to learn from the way congregations and ministers in small churches perform their ministries. Small churches often do engage in prophetic ministry. But this is not the main point of this book. This book's main point is that ministries in small churches, whether prophetic or not, have something to teach the whole church, precisely because such ministries take place in churches that are not large. Through these reflections we may discover insights about ministry that perhaps have escaped us, or assumptions about ministry that need revision. Such discovery is a clear implication of the parable, and it would be inadvisable to disregard the mustard seed altogether.

This book is not mainly a how-to or inspirational book. There are many excellent works of that type available, of which a number are listed at the end of this book. The contributions in this book do offer advice and inspiration. The primary purpose of this book, however, is to present reflections by pastors themselves, pastors currently engaged in small church ministry, on who they are and what they are doing. This book presents voices of the pastors. It comes straight from the practitioner.

These are reflections on the way it is by those who do it. They grew out of my asking a selection of small-church ministers in a variety of situations to think honestly about their lives and work. What they describe and reflect on is ministry as it is, as seen by ministers in terms of their expertise instead of that of the teacher, supervisor, or consultant. The voices

5

here represent men and women, younger and older, more experienced and less, lively and humdrum, and people to the east, west, north, and south (the majority from the Midwest and West). Some are recently out of seminary, others approaching retirement, and others are in between. One is in postretirement, a not uncommon situation. The more conservative and less conservative are represented here.

These reflections do not lend themselves to generalizing. The one thing they demonstrate as a whole is the variety of responses to the distinctive concerns and issues of small churches, usually in rural areas. Certain themes do recur. Intimacy typically extends widely in the small church congregation. Pastoral calling is often done as a matter of course. The pace of ministry seems more relaxed than what might be assumed in seminaries and staff churches. Ministers in small churches usually have more time for reading than in larger churches. The small congregation is often more nearly a genuine family, as a whole, when small enough for that to be possible. Ministers in small churches are often the ministered to. What changes over time in small churches is less the church than the minister.

These reflections furthermore show the changes in ministers' attitudes to ministry that can occur in small church settings. There is a pronounced interest in the minister's "I" in these essays, which may be a result more of the circumstances of their solicitation than of the small church. At the same time, the "we" in these essays almost always means "I and the people I minister with," rather than the church staff or denomination.

Such recurrent themes illuminate ministry. I think, however, that what readers will find here is not so much source material for characterizing the small church in general as a mirror of ministry in which to examine themselves and their ministry with a view to insight and renewal. Readers will be affected in different ways, as they discover their places in the shade of the mustard plant. In the end, the subject is not ministry in the small church but ministry in itself.

These reflections are from the minister's perspective. It would be desirable someday to see a comparable collection of reflective essays by nonministers in small church congregations.

■ 1 ■

"You're Moving Where?"

Jane Newstead

I CAN'T COUNT the number of times I answered those questions as I prepared to leave San Francisco for Odebolt, Iowa. "That's right. Odebolt. Natives pronounce it 'O-dee-bow.'"

For a full year before I arrived in Iowa, all we heard of in California about the Midwest was the devastating effect of the farm crisis. Friends couldn't believe that I would voluntarily move to Iowa. But then six years earlier I had left a law practice in southern California to move to seminary, so why should a move to Odebolt occasion surprise?

Where? Odebolt is a community of about a thousand people in northwest Iowa. It is seventy miles east of Sioux City, eighty miles from the nearest interstate and airport. We're not really in the middle of nowhere—it just looks that way on the map. We are in the middle of incredibly beautiful corn and soybean fields. Miles and miles of the richest farmland in the nation. And the fields are always beautiful, whether lush with the green of the newly sprouted crops, full of brown stalks waiting for the combine, or bare and covered with winter snow. The sunset on the horizon each clear day is a reminder of God's creative imagination and of the rich blessings God has given us.

And people respond. In Odebolt there are five churches, each with two hundred to three hundred members from town and the surrounding area. The church members are farm families, retired farmers, widows, some school teachers, several small business owners and bankers, and employees of the grain elevator. Everyone here is dependent on farm income in one way or another. There is no other industry in town. Virtually

JANE NEWSTEAD *was pastor of First Presbyterian Church in Odebolt, Iowa. She is now pastor of St. Andrew Presbyterian Church in Aptos, California.*

everyone belongs to a church. "I'd like you to meet Sally. She's a Methodist," (or Lutheran, or whatever) runs the typical introduction.

The churches in town all belong to established denominations: Missouri Synod Lutheran, Evangelical Lutheran Church of America, United Methodist, Presbyterian, and Roman Catholic. The school superintendent joins the ministers for our monthly ministerial association meeting. The United Methodists, ELCA, and Presbyterians conduct a joint vacation Bible school, midweek Lenten services, and Good Friday services. The Catholics join us for Thanksgiving evening and World Day of Prayer. Two churches in town have had to close in the last fifteen years. Our members recall when we had over 300 members, ten years ago. We now have 209 on our rolls. The town has lost over 500 residents during the same period. Sections of land that formerly supported fifteen to twenty people in three or four households now support two people in one home.

Why Odebolt? I looked for a call in a place like Odebolt because I knew I did not want to be an associate in a large church. I looked at the employment statistics for women in the Presbyterian church and realized that my best chance was for a small church in the Midwest. Churches I interviewed with were skeptical. I had lived all my life in cities, had six years of graduate school, am single and female. Ninety-five percent of the members at Odebolt were willing to take a chance, and I liked the town and loved the almost total absence of cars in the streets. Rush hour is from 7:45 to 8:00 A.M., September through May, when the teenagers drive up Walnut and Maple to the school.

How long will you stay? That's the question I hear most frequently. I'm not sure what the answer is. Life here has been miserable and wonderful in about the same proportions as anywhere else. It is just that different things trigger these emotions and occasionally different skills are needed to cope.

■ I ■

Being new in a place is wonderful. It gives you the freedom to hide all the Easter lilies before anyone else comes into the

sanctuary on Palm Sunday and honestly explain later to outraged members that you thought they must have been delivered
early by mistake. It gives you the freedom to speak freely in
trustee meetings until someone tells you a year later that "until
you came the ministers never said anything!" By then it is too
late to change the new pattern.

All change is threatening to a congregation, however. Never
is the truth of the saying that one person's meat is another's
poison more apparent than when change, major or minor, is
suggested in a small church.

When I had been at Odebolt for ten months, we held our
annual officers' training course. Because I had heard much
mumbling about all the changes during the preceding year,
and enthusiasm for several changes that hadn't occurred, the
theme of our meeting was "change." We began by listing all
the changes we could think of, done or undone, without la-
beling them good or bad. I learned a lot. One woman recognized that we now had a "unisex" God, although I had
never talked about inclusive language, and our hymns still carry
all the masculine images. A man stated that he had all the old
prayers of confession memorized and now found a new one
in the bulletin each week. I hadn't known until that moment
that five standard prayers of confession had been used consistently for the past twenty years or more. I thought people
noticed only the Big changes they talked about, like the increasing deacon responsibilities and the written treasurer
reports.

As I looked at the lengthening list of changes, finally about
thirty in all, I understood the sense of uneasiness in this place,
where everything was supposed to be safe and unchanging.
Then we moved on to the things people wanted to change.
Everyone in the room was in favor of making at least one of
the eight or nine significant changes on the list. We had trouble
deciding which to take on first.

It is a truism, but nonetheless true, that the best thing about
living in a small town is that we all know each other. It is
impossible to make a quick trip to the grocery store without
stopping to visit with someone. On a summer evening walk

to the drive-in eight blocks away, you would probably be invited to sit and visit on several front porch steps.

It is also true that the worst thing about living in a small town is that we all know each other. About five months after I moved here, it became apparent that I would have to buy a new car. I talked to the dealer in town, and the evening before my vacation began I took delivery of one. The next day I left town in the car at 5:00 A.M. and a week later returned in it about midnight. The following day, as I was weeding my tomato patch, a man I hadn't met before stopped to introduce himself and ask how I liked my new Plymouth Horizon. I looked over my shoulder to see if it had somehow escaped from the garage. It hadn't. I was amazed to realize people actually read the list of new car registrations published in the local paper. I thought they just filled space. I have recently started taking an occasional peek at the list of moving vehicle traffic violators.

One of the joys of small-town living is knowing each other and caring about each other. People know about the details of everyone else's lives because most people in town are related to each other in some way. At memorial services the family gathers in the church for a prayer before the service begins. It is not unusual for fifty to seventy "family members" to follow the casket into the sanctuary. People ask nosey questions and remember histories and share information about each other mostly because they are concerned and interested, not to be malicious.

One of our troubles is that we know each other too well. As we sit in meetings, we all know before anyone speaks who will be for and who against an issue. We know we can count on Harry to explode anytime a proposal is presented for spending money on anything except the building. We know which members can be counted on to support proposals concerning special offerings and mission projects, and who will keep silent and not vote and then go out and tell the neighbors what awful things we are doing.

In this kind of environment, new ideas frequently are still-born. The moment a proposal is put forward, someone is bound to say, "They won't like it." They? Minds are set before pros and cons are presented, and new suggestions too frequently die in adamant silence after one or two courageous attempts at resuscitation from supporters at the table. The worst meeting of my whole life was one in which there were two votes for the motion and seven not voting.

In a small town and small church where everyone knows each other, it is natural to want to be heard and to have opinions respected. Unfortunately, in this town to disagree has too often been interpreted as dislike or disrespect. One of our elders told me after a session meeting that she didn't think we should "fight" like that in the church. It wasn't proper. I thought it had been a good meeting because people had said what they felt on an important question and left as friends. We had a long talk about the need to express opinions honestly and respect the opinions of others. She also thought that anything the minister supported must be right and shouldn't be questioned. I miss the total approval, but . . .

Members in this church feel a strong sense of ownership. Every month or so I'll find someone I didn't expect in or around the building taking care of a squeaking door, a messy cupboard, a singing toilet, and the like. New plants miraculously appear in the flower beds. Our building is well maintained and will remain so because our members and their parents and children have all worshiped here and celebrated the important moments of their lives here. Wall paneling, sanctuary fixtures and furnishings, hymnals, and Bibles were all given in memory of someone's relatives and are respected and preserved. Even when such gifts have outlived their usefulness, they cannot be discarded or replaced, because "It's a memorial."

A small church has limited storage space. One week I asked the women's group to help me clean out one of the large cupboards to make room for Christian education supplies. There was only one volunteer. We worked an entire morning taking everything out of the cupboard and putting back only those things that had actually been used in recent memory. We had three tables of things left over. By Sunday, when the trustees met to decide what to do with these things, only half a table of items was left. Everything else had been carefully tucked away in other nooks and crannies by people who were sure "We'll need it someday."

There is also a strong interest in how the church is run. Until recently an unwritten rule required that any project costing more than five hundred dollars be approved by the whole congregation. The limit was only recently raised to a thousand. The congregation also approved the budget each year—until I failed to put it on the agenda for my first annual meeting and then spent hours explaining to everyone who called and came in why it wasn't there.

I have struggled many times with the issue of why the congregation's elected elders are reluctant to make decisions on issues without a congregational vote. And I have agonized over the need of the congregation, after the elders have studied an issue and made a decision, to rehash, second-guess, and work at finding ways to get around their decision. I don't have answers, but I suspect that it has something to do with the church being the only place where most of our members have a place to speak up and a right to expect others to take notice. The men farm alone or with brothers, father, or sons. Few of the women work outside their homes. The church is felt to be an integral part of most families' lives—even for some who do not attend regularly or make significant contributions. A person may be elected to the board of the Cattlemen's Association or the Tuesday Club, but important as these organizations are, and as time-consuming as they may be on a short-term basis, they do not compare with the investment of time, energy, love, commitment, and history individuals have in their churches.

Every church member is an "expert" or long-term volunteer in some aspect of the church's work. Each knows "how things should be" and wants them "done right." It is their money that keeps the doors open, and they have a personal interest in seeing that it is properly used. The church is too important to leave to someone else. I am delighted that this is so. However, people are bound to disagree occasionally, and tempers sometimes flare. I see a disturbing pattern of people in all the churches here withholding regular offerings to express disapproval of a particular policy or decision and giving money to the church only for specific building repairs they support.

This need to control, arising from an exaggerated self-importance and need to be heard, is not edifying. Christ has called us as individuals to be members of the body of Christ. Our salvation, in this life and the next, is in and through the members of Christ's body. None of us is called to be an "individual disciple." Indeed, the phrase is an oxymoron. As disciples we are called both to follow and to call others to follow, tasks we cannot accomplish individually. We count on the witness of the church through the ages to lead us, and we are the ones who will lead those who follow us. To distrust those who share our journey is to declare not only that we are the only correct interpreters of the Word in our time and place—an arrogant attitude—but also that only we are capable of making good decisions. God's spirit has been idle and moved no one else.

■ **II** ■

It is wonderful in the church to know that year after year, through thick and thin, Marge will still be teaching kindergarten on Sunday morning. It was not so wonderful to discover that the man who had been teaching the high school class for twenty years had not used the curriculum for the last ten years and instead had been teaching doctrine learned in a weekday Church of God Bible study class. He was also an elder and chair of the Christian Education Committee. And how do you ask the faithful treasurer of the last twenty-five years, who has turned in only one written report per year, incomplete and inaccurate at that, to resign, when she is mother, sister, aunt in six other families in the congregation?

Long-term volunteers are both a blessing and a curse. Life is made easier when we don't have to search for new volunteers for church school, vacation Bible school, annual dinners, ushers, and so on. It is nice not to have to explain always what needs to be done when, where to find resources, and how to get reimbursed for expenses. But it also means that relative newcomers in the congregation (we have no *real* newcomers) have no place to "fit" and have to wait to be asked to substitute.

People who have tired of a job frequently feel unable to leave it and would have no place else to exercise their talents in the church if they did. Almost everyone has an unofficial (frequently unchangeable) label: artist, music, kitchen help, repairs. Stewardship of my time in this area and of congregational talents is an issue I haven't yet resolved.

In many ways the issues during my time in Odebolt have concerned power and authority—theirs, mine, and Scripture's. Mostly these issues have surfaced over the question of how we manage and spend our money—everything from who counts it to whether or not we will increase our mission giving. But the larger question we are unable to address so directly is who we are and what we should be. Opinions range from (a) a place to meet and sing the old favorite gospel hymns on Sunday morning to (z) a people dedicated to serving other people. I don't expect we will come to a common statement of our mission in the next few years no matter how many times we raise the question. The next time I look at a Church Information Form, I'll trust the mission giving pattern, not the mission statement.

In the meantime, the question that colors all our issues is, "Can these bones live?" No, we are not yet dried up and scattered in the desert, but the fear we all hesitate to articulate is that we will be in twenty or thirty years. In three years there have been two baptisms in the church and two weddings (both couples moved out of the area). In one two-week period last fall, we had five services of witness to the resurrection. But we called them funerals. It is easy here to think of the end of this life as being *the* end, even though we know and hope and pray for the life promised in Christ.

In our life together we have a tendency to look only at today and, seeing no way we can save ourselves, we look forward to our "funeral" in much the same way as we are now silently and secretly preparing for the service for our organist, which will certainly take place in the next month or so. We no longer pray for her life, only for her peace and freedom from pain. I make the same prayer daily for this church: for its peace and freedom from the pain we have intentionally and unintentionally inflicted on each other in the past. But I pray too that the Spirit will once again breathe life and vision and hope for a real future into these bones.

I have found three things essential for me to survive and to thrive in a small town. One, a way and the means to leave town for study, vacation, or committee work for at least one week every three months. This brings all life's challenges back into perspective. Two, an openness about who I am and what I am about. This helps allay idle speculation and tends to slow gossip. I announce plans for vacation, visits of family and friends, and other unusual events in my life in groups of people wherever it is appropriate, so as many people as possible get the same story at the same time and can later correct each other's misinterpretations. Three, a sense of humor, especially a willingness to laugh at my own situation, mistakes, and expectations. A weekly lectionary study group of ministers in the area has helped me keep perspective between trips out of town and has nurtured my ability to laugh when I'm too tired to care. Long distance calls, an answering machine, and two cats who help lower my blood pressure when life gets out of hand are also essential.

So how long will I stay? Probably only as long as I can still laugh at myself and at the absurdities and delights of rural life. And that will probably be as long as there are ministers to meet with on a regular basis for Bible study and one or two friends who listen to me and laugh with me. And until the congregation gets tired of putting up with all the change.

■ 2 ■

Shrink to Fit?

Chandler Stokes

I WAS BORN in the suburbs, where the middle class grows its hippies. Although I was raised going to Sunday school, I became increasingly disaffected with the church as I grew from rebellious teenager to educated adult. My university training didn't address all of my questions, so I tried music and then religion. I worked as a folksinger in nightclubs and bars before entering seminary. I met my wife, Karen, at seminary. We got married and got ordained. We now co-pastor two small churches in northern California and have two small children. I want to reflect about issues related to the growth of one of our churches, Community Presbyterian Church in Garberville.

Garberville is on the Eel River two hundred miles north of San Francisco along Highway 101. The people in the post office know your name, and you know theirs. The local paper comes out once a week. It tells you almost nothing about events outside the county and more than you may want to know about things inside the county. You may have heard of Garberville, maybe because of the fishing or the redwoods, but probably because of the Emerald Triangle—notorious for growing marijuana—of which Garberville is the center. There are about five thousand souls in and around Garberville, and they have been generally divided into two groups. The people who came to the area during the back-to-the-land movement of the 1960s and 1970s and who tend to live in the hills (and only some of whom grow marijuana) are called the counterculture. The more longtime residents who are in lumber, tourism, or real estate represent the mainline culture. The divisions between these groups are really not very clear. In fact, the lines

CHANDLER STOKES *is co-pastor of Community Presbyterian Church in Garberville, California, and Leggett Presbyterian Church in Leggett, California.*

of division are getting fuzzier as the town's children all go to school and grow up together.

We started work here three and one-half years ago. Just under thirty people came to worship on Sunday mornings, and, as might be expected, none of those who attended could be easily identified with the counterculture. After our struggling to get our feet on the ground in the ministry, experimenting with various styles of co-pastoring, and learning to call upon the strength of the church's leadership, attendance crept up over thirty two well into our ministry. Over the next year it slowly increased to just over forty adults with six children in worship. Now suddenly in the last couple of months there are closer to sixty adults and fifteen children coming on Sunday.

I find this both gratifying and unsettling. For someone who was once interested primarily in the meaning of life, I have to come to grips with that last paragraph about numbers in church. That having more people in church makes me feel good I find somewhat distressing. It makes me nervous and skeptical. I want to understand why this is happening and what righteousness and unrighteousness are hidden in our "success."

■ I ■

According to people with a lot of experience in these matters, very small churches don't grow. Very small means under thirty-five in attendance on Sunday. So what is happening in Garberville?

Almost any session or nominating committee who invites you to a "small, struggling church" will tell you that they want their church to grow. The people who asked us to come here genuinely wanted to increase membership. To be willing to grow is to be willing to change, and people here knew that in some way, too. Even though growth and change here are new, there still seems to be a willingness—here before we came—to face these realities.

When you're looking for a job, there is very little to tell you whether people mean it when they say they want to grow. We had at least two indications that they did here: we were younger than the youngest people in the church, and we demonstrated a positive outlook toward the counterculture. And still they said, "Come," knowing, or at least guessing, that if we came, and the church grew, the church would surely change.

■ II ■

The longtime members of this church are a lot like my parents, and the people who are recently coming to church are a lot like me. Probably the most important thing that gave me liberty to enter into the established church community was that during seminary I came to know my parents as adults. I have the good fortune of healthy relationships with both, respect for their issues, and some understanding of their pain. Those relationships have shed light on the people I pastor. It has given me access to the most holy ground of the church—these people's lives.

Once I gained entry to the community, it was for me to see that the door stayed open for others. For new people to find their way in they need to find a point of access, a doorway into the church. The people who have recently started coming to church are more like me than the longtime members, especially when it comes to church. We, newcomers, are a little uneasy with the institution but are looking for some way to relate seriously to God. Like a lot of them, I had tried to develop that relationship without a community, structure, or the burden of the institution, but found that to be a deceptive path. When Karen and I came to Garberville, my uneasiness with the institution was apparent, though my committed relationship to it was pretty apparent too—both would have been hard to hide, even if I had tried.

One way to describe my relationship to these two worlds (one "inside" the church and one "outside" the church) is to say that where I reside most consistently is in the "doorway" of the church. It feels a lot like lying down on the job. I mean we haven't done that much. Maybe it's what some people call a ministry of being. That's in part why it's gratifying to see more people in church: I can count them and the count is changing.

"Lying down in the doorway" has some hazards. It helps keep the door open, but can anyone get by you? I once heard of someone who had that problem. It was said he had lots of good friends outside of the church, but none of them became a part of the church. So far that hasn't been the problem for us. Our trouble, if you want to call it that, is keeping our friends out of the church. It has always been important to us to maintain friendships outside the institution. Most of our old friends—the "golden" ones—aren't related to the church. Most of our new friends are finding their way into it. It may be that I am moving further inside the doors of the church myself and may be losing my position in the doorway.

Another hazard is that people are coming to the church largely through us. People are becoming part of the church because we are the pastors. Instead of being in the door, we are the door. If our leaving prompts a lot of other folks to leave, we have turned the church into a personality cult and have failed in a serious way. Under these circumstances, it is difficult to judge your effectiveness before you're gone. Keeping the door open seems to be easy. Keeping out of the way is a little trickier. Getting people to encounter one another within the church and develop relationships with one another and apart from you is essential to building up the body as opposed to the numbers.

In a church this size almost everyone becomes a kind of friend to the pastors, because sooner or later lives will enter some crisis and members and pastors will emerge closer to one another. It is a great beauty of small churches that pastors get to develop relationships with almost everyone. And it looms as a potential trap on the way to a congregation's and a pastor's spiritual growth.

One of the crises that keeps showing up and drawing us closer to people new to the church is expressed in this way: "I think I might actually believe in God, and I like what's happening in church, but I'm not so sure I want to become a Christian, join the church, and all that."

The following scenario is not uncommon among newcomers to the church. They had some contact with the church when they were children, grew up, learned to think, went to college (where in today's world they learned that tradition was bunk— well, that's what *I* went to college to learn), left all that religious mumbo-jumbo behind, became adults, and then somewhere in that process their questions about meaning and purpose seeped to the surface and became explicit. That or a similar story is told by more than half of the new people coming to church. Others come "because of the kids," but decide to stay "for ourselves." The story of those who come for their kids differs from the first only in that it is their children who have become the focus of their questions of meaning, value, and purpose.

Others come because another church has asked them to check their intellect at the door, and the wound has begun to bleed. Others for some doctrinal reason. Others because we have just about the only church choir in town. Others because Karen and I are a clergy couple, and they're curious. The persistent theme in these people's stories, though, is that what they remember or have experienced as the traditional church has left them feeling incomplete. The church has failed to make contact with their truly religious questions.

■   III   ■

The two primary doorways into the church in Garberville are Sunday worship and inquirers' groups. People who haven't been in church for a long time, or ever, tend to find church language puzzling, or problematic, or just opaque. The inquirers' group (which came to be known as the "Heathens and Heretics" because everyone felt like one or the other) came into being as an opportunity for people to talk about the religious language used in worship, the buttons it pushes and the baggage it carries, to talk about stumbling blocks in the way of entering Christianity.

We talk theology for hours and hours, meeting month after month. People come with unending questions about the Bible, sexist and formulaic language, meditation, baptism, eucharist, healing, and most anything else. People come with resources as well as questions. Often church members will come along to "Heathens and Heretics" to pursue their questions and bring their resources to the conversation. Our role as pastors is to interpret the tradition as it makes sense to us. We try to make room for people to find their way into the tradition—and that is easy in the Reformed tradition. The theological breadth of the church is a tremendous asset in helping people find a link between themselves and the tradition.

Some of those who come to the inquirers' groups end up joining the church, but not all. There are some who have been coming ever since the groups began, and still their journeys have not led them to church membership. But almost all of those who join the church come by baptism and affirmation or reaffirmation of faith.

With the first group of inquirers (of whom four became new members of the church), four or five months were spent talking about the traditional words used as a profession of faith when people join the church: Jesus Christ is my Lord and Savior. The way that language has been used and abused, these words have become a serious stumbling block to those trying to find their way in, and yet are an inexhaustible source of dialogue. Those who were finding the church an inescapable part of their lives decided that, when they joined the church, they wanted to affirm these traditional words but also didn't want to let these words stand alone. Since then, it has become a tradition that upon joining new members are invited to confess their faith in their own words using the traditional formula.

One of those first personal statements came from a doctor in town who said, "When I say Jesus is Lord, that means the image of Jesus is more powerful than the image of a gun. And when I say that Jesus is my Savior, that means that when I get rocked to the center of my being, I come here to sing and cry. Now, these words might mean something different tomorrow, but that's what they mean to me today."

Another, the town's librarian, who says he used to delight in heaping derision on Christians, said:

"There comes a time in life when we are forced to admit the truth: I have missed the mark. In my weakness I cannot continue alone.

"We realize that we have been swollen with pride, driven by a relentless and merciless ego. But in time pride drains away like a stream in summer, and the once-mighty ego is reduced to impotent rantings. It stands revealed not as the center of our being but as a millstone round the neck. And we are left with a bleak perception of our world.

"We realize that the good things which have come to us in life are, like grace, undeserved.

"The only real solution to this is love, love focused and personified in Jesus Christ. That unknowable, unfathomable, indefinable mystery which we have the temerity to address as God may be approached through his beloved son and our Lord and Redeemer, Jesus.

"In the unity of the Holy Spirit a circle is formed—a circle of love—between us and Jesus and with each other. Love uniting all humans as brothers and sisters in the mystical body of Christ. A love which is both a gift and a duty. Love thy neighbor as thyself."

For the last two years we have received new members on Pentecost Sunday. This is our way of celebrating Christians' hearing the Spirit "each in their own language." Personal statements of faith have become an explicit witness in worship to that hearing. Of course, not everyone wishes to say more than the traditional confession. But whenever these statements are shared, they become a high point of the church year. These confessions have a power to speak doubts and convictions in a way that has led me to use them at other times of the year as communal confessions of faith.

I mention these people's occupations because it then becomes obvious that they have significant formal education. Though people with formal education may not be common in every small church, they are in this church. Here school teachers, educators, and other professionals (working and retired) make up the majority. We may be the only church in town trying to provide a home for a thinking faith, which may be the role of many Presbyterian churches in rural North America.

The education of these people makes a difference in the way we conduct worship. With the stumbling block biblical literalism represents for people, reading the Scripture from the RSV without setting a context for the reading is practically pointless, except for those who are truly biblically literate— and how many Presbyterians do you know who are biblically literate? So we usually do an exegesis or explanation of some kind before the reading of Scripture to attempt to provide a meaningful context for its hearing.

There is at least one person in the church who objects to this style of Scripture reading. She has a more conservative view of Scripture, approaching literalism, and I don't agree with her much, but obviously I want to keep the conversation going with her. Seeing that everyone is included in the conversation is one of the best things about Presbyterian community, and I don't want to violate that with my agenda for opening the doors.

I guess I really don't know what to do except talk with her about it. I think that in general people don't really care that much about doctrinal matters. When folks present a theological concern, they are usually disclosing a personal pain. The process of the inquirers' groups, for example, tends to start with the issue of religious language, but it is the pain of finding there is no room for them in the language, the religion, or the community that is the real personal issue. (Calling the groups "Heathens and Heretics" is a playful way of revealing that pain.) In many cases it is the willingness of members of the institution to sit and listen to "outsiders' " questions, concerns, and pains that helps open the doors of the church, and not so much talking about accessible theology (though that doesn't hurt).

We are a church that has entered into significant dialogue with the unchurched, and we have discovered that this dialogue has become a very busy bridge. This is not only carried on in inquirers' groups but also in worship. Besides addressing people's intellectual needs and experiential roadblocks in our manner of presenting Scripture, we also take particular care in providing a context for other parts of the liturgy. It is sometimes difficult to achieve a balance between explaining the liturgy and letting people get taken up by the liturgy, but when the balance works it's another bridge to the outside.

The variety of theological views in the Presbyterian church has given rise to a strange phenomenon: we tend to be accepting of people's theological views as long as we don't know what their views are. As long as people look more or less the same, they are easy enough to accept, but don't let them say what they really think. What we have now in the Garberville church are people who look quite different from one another and yet who are finding mutual acceptance. Now the depth of that acceptance will be tested as the ongoing conversation reveals what individuals really think. The conversation has begun partly through the public statements of faith in worship and partly through the openness of a few people in the church. The changing aspect of growth is just coming to fruition. In the best situations, I have heard people from the counterculture and people in the mainstream say, "Church is more meaningful to me when I know how different my views are from the people next to me and at the same time realize that we are all coming to the same well to drink." In small communities every conflict is major, and having these worlds of the mainstream and the counterculture meeting in church is full of potential for conflict. But these things really are said and seem to happen when people talk to one another. Constant dialogue looks like a good idea in this ministry.

■ **IV** ■

Besides the "thinking faith" that nearly everyone in the congregation craves, there is one more aspect of Reformed faith that cuts through the social distinctions. "God alone is Lord of the conscience." More than any other theologoumenon in the tradition, this is the one that people can articulate and that they prize.

Who are the people who live in the country? In our part of rural North America, the people who were born here are here because their parents came to work in the tourist or lumber industries. Their parents came because they didn't care much for city life: too much government, too many people, too much society, too many constraints. The children stay in part because they agree. They are rugged individualists like their parents.

The people who move here now don't come for economic reasons. They come here to retire, or to get back to the land, or to get away from the mainstream culture. Except for the retirees, there is a common thread in all of these motivations. People move to the country to get away from group pressure and authority. Some people who live in the country like to have this tendency balanced by a fundamentalist church in their religious life. But this is not for everyone.

"God alone is Lord of the conscience" means everyone doesn't have to agree, not even with the preacher, or an elder, or the majority. Contrary to popular belief, people don't move to the country for peace, unity, and purity. Peace, maybe. Purity, maybe. But unity only if it doesn't violate "God alone is Lord of the conscience." Now that's Presbyterian, country Presbyterian. Of course there are obvious distortions lurking in this view, but it is a potent place to begin a dialogue.

There's another thing that these people share despite cultural differences. They all feel a little ambiguous about being so far from where things are happening. Most people in North American churches are quite remote from the border zones of war and poverty, and sometimes we feel that remoteness. We feel far away from the seats of power and influence. In the country these feelings are intensified, because in some way we have all chosen to be a little more out of touch with the mainstream. We don't see the massive industry that moves the economy or its far-reaching effects.

■ V ■

It is easy to let the world be small in Garberville. It is just as easy to let God shrink to fit.

So, the church is growing, and it feels good. Maybe in time lay leadership will grow and relationships will be strengthened between the two worlds in Garberville. I feel like Richard Pryor with his free-base pipe. His good friend Jim Brown, after each good thing Richard has to say about his drug habit, is (like my conscience) repeating his litany, "Whachou gawn do?"

"There's all these people coming to church."

"Whachou gawn do?"

"They accept each other."

"Whachou gawn do?"

"They *love* each other."

"Whachou gawn do?"

I think about my own life and how hard it has been to live responsibly in relation to hungry, marginalized, victimized, oppressed, and dying people, and I wonder if all of this amounts to a hill of beans. I don't even have a plan.

I preach to the limits of my vision. I don't think the church's growth is due to a watering down of the message to uplift the poor. I think these people would feel lied to if we let them think anything less than that was expected of them. I keep preaching that vision in hopes that somehow we will together find a way there.

Two of our members left for the Peace Corps. Maybe Habitat for Humanity or something like that is my personal solution, but I went into parish work because I thought that something responsible could happen here. I guess I still do. And maybe having the church grow is instrumental to our finding a responsible path. Maybe in the building and growing of these communities there will arise not only a vision but a highway for our God.

It's so easy to get distracted. It's so similar to what I thought it was like when I was a kid—they all talk about that stuff on Sunday, but what are they doing the rest of the week? Only now I'm them.

We've raised our mission giving the last two years. We raised a thousand dollars for One Great Hour of Sharing. Another thousand went through the deacons' fund. The two-cents-a-meal program is going well. We have an emergency food program and clothing room. It is not an entirely bleak landscape. It's just that it is easy to let the world be small in Garberville. It is just as easy to let God shrink to fit.

■ 3 ■

The Work Is God's

Dorothy Price Knudson

ST. JOHN'S CHAPEL by the Sea is in mission territory. When it was built in 1962, that was not the case. At that time forests were being logged, shake mills were busy, and tourists jammed the beaches to dig razor clams in season. There was enough work to support many families. The town had a movie theater and was self-sufficient enough that trips to "town" (Aberdeen) were not the necessity they have now become. The tide of change, however, has left just a handful of people. Houses belonging to year-round residents want repair, and their yards go untended. Second homes of part-time residents are generally better cared for—evidence of more money and more energy there, it seems.

Hunger is not just an issue people encounter elsewhere. A mother told me how her family "diets" in the winter when work is scarce. Among the few children who attend church school are two who like toast and peanut butter at my house before they go because they haven't had breakfast.

In an atmosphere of malaise and despair, among the favorite recreational activities are sex, alcohol, and drugs. There are many young mothers, married and single, who lack most skills for childrearing. We are close to the Quinault Nation Reservation in Taholah, twelve miles north. As most realize, alcohol is a significant problem for Native Americans. So far, St. John's has been selected for a couple of weddings and receptions for tribal members because alcohol is not allowed in the building. Rumors of drug traffic in the grade school arise from time to time, and I am told one of the boys came to worship high on marijuana or something else. He's nine.

DOROTHY PRICE KNUDSON *was pastor of St. John's Chapel by the Sea in Pacific Beach, Washington. She is now pastor of Mount Baker Presbyterian Church in Concrete, Washington.*

The main Christian church in Taholah is connected with the Pentecostal movement. A mother brought her daughter to St. John's because we did not emphasize demon possession and protecting children from satanic toys. Since the native Shaker-like religion is caught up in concerns of spirit possession, one can understand the compatibility of Pentecostalism. A nurse told of a woman who had a stroke while eating chicken. The Shaker ministers tried to coax the spirit of the chicken out of her body.

The only other active church in Pacific Beach itself is an independent fundamentalist church where the pastor stresses the value of spankings in correcting children who don't do what their parents want. As the pastor of the Pacific Beach Gospel Chapel is also a grade school principal, he carries his philosophy over into his school job. The church and elementary school are next door to each other, and a number of teachers who share his theological outlook have been hired at the school. Most of the parents are school dropouts who experienced little academic success. They found jobs in the woods and restaurants or bars rather than continuing their educations. They did not know how to manage in the educational system as students, nor do they as parents, so it is understandable that there has been no public outcry from even those parents who don't think corporal punishment is the best way to respond to behavior problems in children.

Signs advertising burls for sale are spelled "burrols." Nobody seems to care. Too many children say, "I'm in the second grade but should be in the fourth." As I talk with them I find them of at least average intelligence. One mother told the teacher that she did not want her son held back. The boy made passing grades or better but "preferred playing to working." The mother is a navy wife and is rare in not being tied permanently to the community. She was thus willing to question the school's policy, which may needlessly damage a child's self-esteem. Other children are not so lucky, while the schools themselves are in a difficult position.

People have had too many murders and suicides in their families to have much energy. I know mothers of convicted killers and children whose parents, aunts, uncles, and grand-parents have died through either suicide, murder, or both. If ever there was a place that needs to hear good news preached, this is the place. Attendance has risen from five when I first appeared to an average of twenty to twenty-five occasionally swelling to thirty or thirty-five. A 500 percent increase looks good on paper, but we still have not reached critical mass. The elders are elderly. We just celebrated the eighty-eighth birthday of one. Another elder is good-hearted but not equipped to deal effectively with polity. There is only one family in the whole congregation, two parents and two children. Other children come alone. I'm their taxi service. On occasion I have even played the piano for the worship service. I have been here two and one-half years, a long time compared with the average six months' tenure of ministers before me. Where there was no church school we now have one, with an average attendance of five children—sometimes two, sometimes twelve.

We have been aided by the Galilean Chapel in Ocean Shores, sixteen miles away geographically but far distant socially—a large, active church in a growing community. We've shared Lenten dramas, classes, and cantatas with Galilean. While Galilean Chapel is a beneficial friend, it is a constant reminder of a going concern. In contrast, St. John's struggles continuously.

■   I   ■

My experience here is quite different from what it would be in a congregation with adequate gifts for the needs of the people, where my job would be to develop their gifts. What I find is that I am in the congregation without support. For these people, perhaps more important than the gospel preached is the gospel embodied. I understand Paul's instructions to the Philippians to imitate him. I am aware that my attitude and behavior are what many people here who never attend worship services will learn of the gospel. I try to convey authenticity and a sense of hope.

Communion at St. John's is served on the second Sunday of the month. All are invited to gather round the table and to share the meal to which they have been invited by Jesus. Steve's response to this invitation is particularly moving. Nine years old and of a dysfunctional family, Steve is not baptized. He would like to "be a part of God," but his mother will not allow it. I do not know why, as Steve's sister is baptized. His mother seems to urge him to go to Sunday school sometimes when he doesn't want to and withholds the privilege other times. Perhaps her need for control in her life comes out in her treatment of Steve. Steve helps other children fold their hands for prayer at the communion table. Later he asks to eat the bread scraps and drink more grape juice. Good news is making its way into his life through the acceptance and welcome he finds at church. Although I have invited his mother to church, things are now at a stalemate. I will have to try again.

Steve has step brothers and step sisters and half brothers and half sisters as well as a full sister, Jenny, who is back home with their mother and her husband once again. She had been with their father and his wife for a while. The children are appealing, and the family situation is fairly typical. Jenny wrote a letter to God asking, "Do you love me?" and asked me to deliver it. I felt it deserved a written response, so I wrote her a letter over my own signature. I assured her that God does love her. She likes to pray and sing in the sanctuary. She is intrigued with the piano. While piano lessons are not a high priority in her family, there are signs that there is money for drugs and alcohol, as the parents are often in the local taverns, and sometimes the children mention they don't feel well or are sleeping Sunday mornings. Our organist has agreed to give Jenny free piano lessons.

Both children are bright and personable. The always-rough journey to adulthood will be even more perilous in their case. Unless the church makes enough of an impact on their lives so that they believe a way of life is possible that is different from that of their parents and too many people they know, Steve and Jenny may waste their lives in the old, familiar pattern. They will become parents in their midteens, and chances are they will not find work other than the low-paying, uncertain work of shake mills, bars, and restaurants. They will be dependent on welfare, and their own children will be known to the Children's Protective Services. Steve tells me, "The kids at school hate me." I hear from other children that Steve is disruptive, and I suspect that he has been spanked often by those teachers who believe that spanking is what God wants done when children don't obey.

After Steve came to church high on marijuana, I informed his mother. She was shocked. "I can't believe it," she said. Yet the community talks of her and her live-in companion as frequent users of both alcohol and marijuana. Perhaps their stash was Steve's source. Presumably it was in retaliation for my visit that she refused to allow him to return. So his sister Jenny and a couple of other children are no longer at church. I will never again talk in this way to the parents of a child in a dysfunctional family. It was a hard lesson. Fortunately, the children have been picked up by the Assembly of God church at Copalis Crossing ten miles east.

■ II ■

I find that my preaching is increasingly an exploration in depth of the meaning of the Scripture readings. People like hearing what the general theme or concern of the whole book is. They like paying attention to the passages that come before and after the lection for the day. They like my tying the morning's Scripture to the assigned Scriptures of the past few weeks. If people cannot or will not come to Bible classes, they will still be presented with the Bible's power. I read all three lections nearly every Sunday and often use the appointed Psalm as a responsive reading. I remember that a former national church leader from our region, John Connor, always read lots of Scripture, believing that it might be all the Bible some people would hear all week. People like hearing the historical and social situation from which the lections come because it makes the Bible as a whole more understandable. They are delighted to learn the biblical meaning of many words society has altered. For example, discovering that to repent means to change my attitude is more helpful than thinking I am supposed to beat myself up emotionally.

The Golden Rule is to love others as ourselves. The reality is that many people in our society don't love themselves much. To love others equally to that isn't much of an honor. Because our whole society is a "putdown" society, self-confidence and self-esteem are under constant threat. Loving oneself has to be emphasized. Good news has to include feelings of increased self-worth, so I've taught classes in improving self-esteem. Classes have not been limited to women, but most of those who attend are women. It has been an area of outreach for the church but may not increase membership, because many of the class members are already active in other churches in Ocean Shores and Aberdeen. It is gratifying to think that these ideas are spreading out beyond St. John's and Pacific Beach.

A couple in a long-term marriage were my only students in one of the self-esteem classes. All three of us enjoyed speaking more positively about ourselves and others. We especially appreciated the freedom that the substitution of the word "could" for "should" brings. The wife credits the class with enabling her to know her husband better than she had in the past. She is not specific about the changes. I think it is because they now have a way of talking to each other without blame, which enables them to share in more depth. As they return to their home church they spread the ideas taught in the class. In rural areas a teacher gets speedy feedback. The husband applies some of what he has learned to other situations. Both have passed some of the ideas on to their grown children and young grandchildren.

In small churches and rural areas there is not a heavy emphasis on formal learning, but teaching packaged in an informal manner can have great impact. I see my students in the post office, café, and grocery store, where we have opportunities to discover whether we're practicing the lessons of the class. One student caught me saying, "I can't add very well," when I went to buy stamps. I changed that to "adding isn't my best thing" before I left the post office. I would guess a minister in a small town is seen in more contexts than in more metropolitan areas. It makes connections between preaching and behavior very visible. A couple in the church know that I get frustrated digging razor clams. It takes me so long to dig the hole out that I don't always believe the clam is way down there. They know, too, how much I like to eat clams.

Having been asked by a member of the Presbyterian Women's group in the Hoquiam church to "help the women feel better about themselves," I had another opportunity to share good news. Since the women have consciously identified with Martha, insights and stories from Elisabeth Wendel-Moltmann, *The Women Around Jesus* (New York: Crossroad, 1982), could be used to give them a new perspective on her. It is Luke who talks about Martha's bustling in the kitchen while Mary chooses "the right thing." A person who has identified with the one making the wrong choice already feels herself to be less than those who've made the right choice. I reminded the women that in John it is Martha who boldly tells Jesus, "Lord, if you had been here my brother wouldn't have died!" She is willing to engage in serious discussion with Jesus while her sister waits at home. And to Martha Jesus reveals that he is the resurrection. From the attentiveness of their gaze and alert posture I could tell they liked hearing that.

They enjoyed the legend of Martha, the dragon slayer, even more. It seems that beginning in the tenth century in the south of France stories were told of Mary, Martha, and their brother, Lazarus, now a bishop, who emigrated to France. Upon their arrival Martha was asked by the people living between Arles and Avignon to slay a dragon who was menacing them. She agreed and upon encountering the dragon placed a cross before him, sprinkled him with holy water, and tied him with her girdle until the people came to kill him themselves. Pictures and statues of the time depict a plump, matronly Martha beside a rather surprised dragon. One statue shows her thrusting a sword into the dragon, but rather than the intent activism of St. George, Martha seems to have her mind elsewhere.

The women particularly enjoyed the interpretation that the feminine method of Martha is to transform rather than the masculine method of George which is to destroy. They did indeed "feel better about themselves." One told me she had always thought of herself as a "latent dragon slayer." I felt privileged to be present as the women in their late sixties and early seventies transformed their thoughts about themselves and Martha.

One of the most powerful effects of the gospel is liberation. Those who have encountered good news feel an expansion of life. They feel confident to attempt tasks they thought were beyond them. They offer love and friendship more readily. They hope for improved relationships and new ways of dealing with problems that have seemed overwhelming. One person tells me how liberating it is to understand "forgive," "repent," "grace," and especially "love" in a new way that brings hope and liberation.

■ III ■

Having been at Pacific Beach more than two and one-half years, I am astounded that I have survived here at the end of the world—literally, the place where land ends, where reception for public radio is minimal, where interest in cultural events or community betterment is almost nonexistent, and where most of those who have skills and abilities have left. There have been real gains in ministry at St. John's and other places— improved marriages, better chances for productive adulthood, higher self-esteem, and more satisfying self-understanding in and among people. People have encountered good news and the task remains enormous.

The continuing irony of my experience at St. John's is that at the same time my gifts are being affirmed, my presence here is questioned. "I didn't think you'd be here so long." "Imagine finding someone like you out here at the beach." So while there have been gains, I find that I am caught up in the American emphasis on success even while we are called to obedience not success. Perhaps all ministry is like St. John's, except the outline is more stark here. In order to supplement the $8,400 salary, I have worked at the local resort as a restaurant hostess evenings. This means I cannot give full-time energy to responding to the need for wholesome recreation for the children and teenagers. I would like St. John's to be a community center where people can learn to share with each other and feel secure enough to ask for help with the problems that all sorts of abuse cause.

In the endless and extreme loneliness, my solace is books. Here I understand the importance of a support community to survival. To be able to discuss art, music, and literature. To be involved with other people discovering more about theology, psychology, and the Bible. To have friends to go out for lunch with. These are longings infrequently fulfilled.

Underlying my experience is a more serious question. To find oneself in such a barren situation means not only to take on alien jobs but to watch gifts and talents remain unused or underused. How do we understand the incompatibility between the gifts God gives and the tasks God presents? Through it all I say the words from Isaiah 46:10-11: "My counsel shall stand, and I will accomplish all my purpose. I have spoken, and I will bring it to pass; I have purposed, and I will do it." The future is in God's hands. The work is God's, the church is God's, and I am God's.

■ 4 ■

God Means Soybeans

David Robert Ord

"I FEEL as if I don't have a pastor." The words were spoken by an agricultural consultant, a member of my congregation, an elder, and the treasurer of the church. I was stunned. He continued, "You don't speak to my needs."

I had worked so hard to be a pastor to these people. Everyone acknowledged that. The "grandfather" of the church had told me repeatedly that they had never had a pastor who had put more effort into his sermons, called on the elderly and sick as regularly as I, been so easy to find when needed, or worked as hard. After all these months of preaching my heart out, did he mean to tell me that everything that was so terribly important to me meant practically nothing to him? After all I had done to serve this church, how could this man who had been on the nominating committee that called me, a pillar of the church, a deeply dedicated man, feel like he didn't have a pastor at all?

Thoughts were coming to me a mile a minute. First there was self-doubt: I was a failure in my first church. Maybe I wasn't cut out for the ministry at all. Though I had just gone through a major career change, I began to have visions of being forced to make another. But at forty, what would I do? I felt like my whole life was going down the tubes. As I pictured myself getting on a plane back to England to seek shelter with my brother, from deep within waves of anger began surfacing. I had been attacked! My next thought was to defend myself, to attack back. It wasn't me, it was these dumb people. What could I expect of ignorant Southern farmers anyway? Soybeans

DAVID ROBERT ORD *was pastor at Trinity Presbyterian Church in Jonesville, Louisiana. He is now pastor at Oak Park Presbyterian Church in New Orleans.*

were all they knew. They had no class. No wonder they were not open to God's vision of justice for all. Why should I waste my time among such small-minded people?

■ I ■

I had emerged from seminary fired with exciting concepts about what God is doing—bringing justice into the affairs of nations. For six months I preached what some of my members jokingly referred to as "cosmos theology." My goal was to give these people the big picture—to enlarge their vision beyond the daily problems of surviving in a dusty Mississippi Delta town. I showed them how God is at work through the evolutionary process, which is pressing for the emergence of a global village. I spoke of a new humanity—of one world in which peace and justice prevail. It was lofty theology. As the woman who was to become my wife would express it a few years later when I played her a cassette recording of one of those early sermons, they were "great college lectures."

When I arrived in Jonesville, my style of speaking attracted people who had not been to church in some cases for years. For one thing, people liked my English accent. As one elder put it, "You get out the crowds." But within six months, the crowds were disappearing. The number in the pews grew fewer and fewer. Finally, we reached crisis point. What was I doing wrong?

Had the conversation ended there, I might never have continued in the ministry. But what this elder said next stuck with me. "All of this theology of the big picture may be important, and you do a good job of it. But you don't speak to my needs. Cosmos theology doesn't relate to my life here in the tough economic times we are going through in Jonesville." He went on to liken my proclamation of the big picture to emptying a lake. "It's all very well for you to keep telling us that we need to keep our eyes on the big picture of emptying the lake," he said, "but that's hard for me to do when I'm hanging onto a limb above the water with alligators nipping at my ass." Suddenly I saw his point of view. I realized that it wasn't intransigence that was the problem, but simply that I was not addressing my congregation in a way they could relate to. Quite simply, I wasn't meeting their needs. My sermons were well thought out, but they didn't touch people's daily lives. It was then that I began to realize that Tillich and Teilhard de Chardin, process theology and liberation theology had to be translated into the language of soybeans.

Soybeans represent the agricultural setting in which Jonesville, population twenty-four hundred, finds itself. Actually, there is a great deal of cotton grown in the region, together with milo, corn, peas, and other crops. But soybeans are the mainstay of the economy.

During the time I served as pastor in this Delta town, the economy was faltering. Poor farm prices had driven many farmers into bankruptcy. A slump in world prices had hurt the oil industry in the Gulf of Mexico, and this in turn ricocheted on our economy, because in its heyday the Gulf furnished employment for not a few people in the town. Not long before I moved here, a garment manufacturing plant closed, throwing scores out of work. The unemployment rate was among the highest in the nation. Jonesville in this period of its history was not the most exciting place in which to begin a ministry. Yet it was the economic woes of central Louisiana that made me the kind of minister I am today.

What people need out of a sermon is help in coping with life from Monday through Friday. They need a lift to get them through the week. Life assaults their dignity, batters their self-esteem—especially in a depressed economy like Jonesville's. But though I learned to speak in the language of the people, I also tried to keep my proclamation of the gospel on the cutting edge of today's thinking. The congregation was stretched and stimulated from week to week, for my preaching still had a lot of thought-provoking content, challenging listeners not to allow their minds to wander. People were getting Tillich, Teilhard, process and liberation theology as much as ever, but in what I tried to make a personal and timely manner. Helping them become all God wants them to be became the focus in place of the cosmos, though the cosmos never disappeared from the fringes. I continued to put into my preaching the amount of preparation and attention to detail that I did with my earlier, more scholarly sermons. Every sermon still received my utmost. Usually sermons were on the boil several weeks before they were served. I like my weekends pressure-free: no Saturday evening preparation for me.

It is not that the church in Jonesville should not be concerned with famine in Ethiopia, injustice in South Africa, or the civil war in Nicaragua. But the principles involved in national and international issues must be adapted to the local environment. I had to begin with what was of concern to them. Then their vision could gradually be expanded. And of primary concern was how the soybean and cotton crops were doing that year.

I found that people in a small town church often lack the buoyant feeling one finds more readily in a large city congregation. Folk boast of their small-town background, but beneath the bravado, they frequently feel inferior, especially when times are tough. People were always apologizing to me for the smallness of Jonesville. My sermons, then, aimed at bolstering their belief in themselves as people loved and accepted by their Creator, regardless of the size of their town and the hard economic times.

It seemed to me that in the minds of many, God was associated more with a certain feeling on Sunday morning than with planting and harvesting soybeans, tending a store, or marketing agricultural products. Using a process mode of theologizing, I tried to show people that there is no division between sacred and secular, between holy and profane—that God is involved in the whole of life, and that the Spiritual Presence permeates every aspect of our world. That means God is interested in soybeans. But God is not a magician in the sky who, if we pray enough, waves a wand and brings us favorable weather patterns. Intervention in the physical creation is not the level of God's involvement in our world. Rather, God is involved in the realm of ideas and possibilities. God inspires within us dreams of what we, our community, and our world can become. God works to release the potential of all humans, to inspire us to make of ourselves all we can be. If old ways of doing things are no longer working, by tuning into God's hopes and dreams for us we can discover new avenues for creative expression.

The people to whom I was preaching were practical folk and, with few exceptions, not particularly philosophical. So I reached them in a practical way: I used stories in my sermons. But I didn't use the typical preachers' stories one often finds in sermon helps. I used secular stories such as those told by Robert Schuller. Nor did I bore people with the typical, "So-and-so in his book on such-and-such tells the story of . . ." I found it much more arresting simply to go straight into the story. I began with a story from the present, raised the issue addressed by the story, and only then delved into the text. I found that beginning with the immediate world, rather than with the world of two thousand years ago, made my preaching more relevant. For instance, one sermon began with the following borrowed story:

A man had spent a lifetime developing an industry that amounted to a two-million-dollar investment. When he was sixty-seven years old, a major fire broke out at the plant. He stood shivering in the winter wind while he watched the fire consuming his property. All he had was two hundred thousand dollars of insurance, and here was two million dollars going up in flames. "Charlie," the man told his son, "call your mother. She's never going to see a sight like this as long as she lives." The plant was a complete loss, and the family was wiped out. Later the entrepreneur's son recalled, "I saw my dad standing there looking at the ashes—sixty-seven years of his life all gone up in smoke. He looked at me and said, 'Charles, there is one wonderful thing about disasters. They burn up all your mistakes. You're free to start again!' " Three months later, Thomas Edison delivered the phonograph to the American marketplace. Out of the ashes of a mistake was born the lighting, the sound system, the heating and cooling we enjoy in this sanctuary today.

On the heels of this introduction to a sermon on how we handle our failures, I raised the issue relevant to my congregation:

All of us make mistakes. We make mistakes in business, mistakes in relationships, mistakes with our children.

Sometimes those mistakes cost heavily. Faced with a failure in our lives, how do we respond? All too often, we indulge in self-blame. We wallow in self-pity. We tell ourselves that we are no good. We see our failure as proof of what we have really always felt about ourselves deep down. It's like the words of a song my roommate used to play a lot when I first moved to New Zealand, "Born to lose."

The sermon went on to contrast Simon Peter's failure with Judas's failure, showing how one forgave himself, picked up the pieces, and, like Edison, made a new start that changed the course of history, while the other couldn't live with his failure and committed suicide.

Much of my preaching tackled the sense of failure that becomes prevalent in hard times. As they watched the economic recovery in other parts of the country, the people in Jonesville felt left out. There was an air of pessimism, a feeling that they were failing as a town. I wanted to inspire hope and courage in the people, and the belief that they could go on even when the bottom dropped out of their lives. I used stories to make my point whenever I could, always finishing with a story that conveyed the point of the sermon in a manner people could remember. Sometimes I would search through books and magazines for hours to find just the right story. But it was always worth it. Stories, I found, grounded the message in everyday life.

■ II ■

It was not only my preaching that changed under the impact of soybeans, but also my understanding of the role of a small church. I went to Jonesville seeking to impose a global vision on a church of seventy or so members, but the shoe didn't fit. It was hard for me to realize that my vision of the church was not their vision, that my goals were not their goals. Instead of trying to get them to see the work God is doing on a global scale, I had to find out where God was already at work among these people. I had to identify God's activity here, learn to believe in and trust it, and make it patent to the people. I could not impose my vision on the church; a vision must emerge from among the people themselves.

Identifying where God was at work in this congregation was no easy matter—not because God wasn't at work, but because my expectations of God's work were so different from theirs. It was not until I had been there about eighteen months that the picture became clear. One evening while chairing a meeting at which we were hammering out the style of worship the congregation related to best, I finally heard the mission of the church articulated. It came from the clerk of our governing body, a lawyer about my own age. He had lived in Jonesville all his life, and he knew the people and their needs. It wasn't the mission I would have chosen as a graduate fresh out of seminary, for at first glance it seemed to have little in common with the thrust of the denomination's national General Assembly. But it was obvious to everyone at the meeting that this was indeed the mission of the church, and I was ready to listen.

What was this mission? Jonesville is located in the Bible Belt. Its population is predominantly Southern Baptist and Pentecostal. In my reading of the situation, to say a person was Baptist in Alexandria or Natchez, our closest central Louisiana larger towns, was not the same as to say a person was Baptist in Jonesville. To be sure, there were moderate Baptists in Jonesville; but the main Baptist church in town had, by our standards, an extremely conservative element. To the minister, the Easter bunny and Santa Claus were taboo. Conservatives had successfully blocked a high school prom dance for many years, and the first was held only as recently as 1987. Here, people take the Bible literally—period. Creation happened in six actual days, and Noah really floated in the ark with all the animals aboard.

In many ways the church I was pastoring had formed its identity over against such fundamentalism. Although a few of our members were lifelong Presbyterians, many had come to us as ex-Baptists. Tired of the narrowness, they had sought a freer expression of their faith. In a real sense, the Presbyterian church was a last chance at religion for some of these people. What members liked most about our church was the fellowship, the freedom to believe according to their conscience, and the opportunity to express their views openly. Had it not been for the existence of a church like ours, they would no longer be in church at all.

Surviving as we did in this sea of fundamentalism, we defined our role as one of receiving people of various persuasions. A few of our members were still quite "Baptist" in some ways. To accommodate them, we used grape juice instead of wine at communion. But we were also careful to guard our freedom, since it was one of the major drawing cards of a church like ours. Most of our members enjoyed a social drink. Every January the younger adult males of the church spent a Friday night playing cards, drinking beer or Scotch, and roasting a pig at a member's camp. And when I visited the church for the first time to consider a call, a churchwide picnic on a member's farm was accompanied by a keg of beer.

The church's mission might not have been one I would have chosen. But what I had overlooked as I entered ministry was that the global concepts I was presenting to this rural Louisiana church did not come to me overnight. They had evolved over the course of several years, during which I had engaged in what for me was deep theological reflection. Yet here I was, expecting people to buy my concepts before they had had the chance themselves to journey on the long pilgrimage that I had undertaken to arrive at my present understanding, or to embark on their own new theological pilgrimage. What seemed obvious to me was not at all obvious to them—nor would it have been to me not too many years ago. I saw now that I had to get involved with people at the point in their pilgrimage at which they found themselves. From this point on, I could relax and get down to the business of giving substance to the church's mission.

The church's sense of what its mission was to be was reflected in the worship. Although they shunned typically Bible Belt taboos and prized the freedom to be themselves, for many the church was nevertheless the one stable institution at a time when everything else was changing. Consequently, worship for these people was associated with a feeling of familiarity and tranquillity. As one young member, the owner of a large oil distribution company, expressed it, "We come to hear a challenging sermon. Otherwise, what we want is that familiar feel that we knew as children. That gets us in a frame of mind to hear the message." To which the chair of the worship committee added, as a commentary on my attempts to introduce nonsexist language, "We don't care what the words of the hymns are. You are probably the only person in the congregation who notices the words at all. It's just not an issue for us." I did, however, continue to model inclusive language in my litany and sermons.

Yet the worship was not staid. The presence of thirty-five children guaranteed that. Within limits, the people were remarkably open to change. They wanted the Lord's Prayer, the Apostles' Creed, and the Gloria Patri in the service because they provided a sense of continuity with the church's past. Beyond that, they had little taste for litany. I do not like to use the Apostles' Creed, and always prefaced it with a statement such as, "Let us confess what we believe using the historic and symbolic words of the Apostles' Creed, written in language we would not use today, yet conveying the truth that God is fully involved in our world, saying together . . ." I have also subsequently found a nonsexist version of the Gloria, from Taizé. Beyond these essentials, the congregation wanted to sing mainly hymns they were familiar with—though they did permit me to use, as long as they were not used all the time, hymns from a supplementary inclusive-language hymnal, copies of which had been purchased for the pews. I also wrote my own words to the Doxology, sung to a new and beautiful tune that the people really liked:

> Praise God from whom all blessings flow,
> Praise God all creatures here below,
> Praise God above each far-flung star,
> Creator, Christ, and Counselor.

And, since they had endured a long period without a minister, they were tired of lay leadership in the service and wanted me to do everything except the children's sermon and the adult and children's choirs.

Theologically, I could have argued with many things, but the lesson that you cannot force people to swallow what they do not have a liking for had sunk in deeply. I knew that all the liturgical and theological correctness in the world could not win against gut feelings. Ministry has meant learning to meet people where they are. To me, the words of hymns are important, but I have learned that I cannot force the issue. As Jesus put it, in straining at a gnat we may swallow a camel. Meeting needs is more important than being correct. Perhaps being correct can come later.

Accepting the people's reluctance to engage in an interactive style of worship, I settled for a thematic worship service in which hymns, prayers, responses, readings, and sermon were all tied together. I prepared a shorter litany than when I first came, but always I wrote my own call to worship, prayer of adoration, prayer of confession, and assurance of pardon afresh. I tried to make them timely, relevant, and in modern language. (Today, I am sold on the thematic approach and the shorter litany and continue to use them in New Orleans.) Traditional liturgical statements such as "Lift up your hearts" were abandoned, and I followed the beautiful style of some of the more up-to-date prayers and meditations found in *Gates of Prayer*, the New Union Prayerbook of the Central Conference of American Rabbis, sometimes borrowing directly, at other times adapting, and frequently writing in a similar vein. Always I was careful to avoid religious-sounding terminology and archaic language, as for instance, in this call to worship:

Why did we come here this morning? We came to worship. To worship is to heighten our awareness of the poetry of our existence. It is to open all the windows of our being to the God who accepts us and in whom we find our home. It is to join the mighty chorus of praise and thanksgiving that has boomed out since the beginning of creation. It is to affirm that we belong—belong to God, to God's world, to all of life. And it is to be transformed into mature, fully alive, truly free people by the impact of God's acceptance of us. Let us worship God.

In similar manner, my prayers of confession, printed in the bulletin and said in unison, avoided religious jargon and built up the individual's worth rather than demeaning him or her, as in the following example:

> Creator of humanity, we admit that we too often have had a low estimation of ourselves. We have not known our worth. And so we have been too quick to believe the negative, too ready to accept limitations, too willing to suffer disappointment. Forgive us for the times we have put ourselves down, as we now forgive those who in days past have put us down.

I also developed my own assurance of pardon, used each week (italicized), with a codicil (roman) that changes from week to week to reflect the particular weakness being confessed:

> *God's pardon is never cheap forgiveness. It is an investment in our growth. God's forgiveness is God's confidence in our ability to change.* In pardoning our low self-esteem, God affirms that we are of inestimable value. In forgiving our poor image of ourselves, God assures us that we are loved. Indeed, God's forgiveness is confirmation of our ultimate worth.

Similarly, the benediction comes in a set form (italicized), with only the specific theme of the day changing from week to week:

> *Go now, remembering that God means you to participate in God's own divinity.* Go, knowing that you are accepted, eternally loved, for the person you are. Go, remembering that God wants you to be your unique self. Go to give of yourself to the world by being all God made you to be. *In the name of the God who created us, the Christ who is our role model, and the Spiritual Presence that is within each of us the spark of divinity.*

The service then concludes each week with the singing of "Let There Be Peace on Earth," with the words slightly modified to read "brothers, sisters, we" instead of "brothers all are we."

So it was that we became a growing church. Of those who stopped coming regularly after my first few months, all but one family returned to the church. By the time I had completed three years, we were adding a new person, invariably in their twenties or thirties, every few weeks. We became one of the few growing Presbyterian congregations in our area.

■ III ■

Meeting people's needs in the manner in which they feel they need to have them met became crucial not only in the pulpit but in other aspects of ministry. I learned to stay in close touch with our lay leadership, responding to their requests joyfully even when it would not have been my choice to take a particular action. And calling. I learned that, appearances to the contrary, everyone has need of their minister. One couple in our church seemed to have it all together. Because they looked so self-sufficient, I called on them little. A year into my ministry, we changed the way we were conducting congregational meetings. It was a change that had been mandated several years earlier when the Northern and Southern churches in our denomination united, but it had never been implemented. The man of the outwardly happy couple was outraged at the change and let his displeasure be known loudly at the back of the church after the service. That afternoon I called on him. We had a frank exchange, during which it emerged that the changes in the congregational meeting were peripheral to the central issues. Far from being self-sufficient, he and his wife were lonely. They had been in this community over twenty years but were still in many ways outsiders. From that point on my whole relationship with them changed, and they became extremely supportive of me. I discovered that every member of a church needs regular visitation.

Whenever problems have arisen, I have not hesitated to meet them head on. No sooner do I hear of a difficulty than I am on the person's doorstep. This was particularly important in a small-town church, where what appeared to me to be a small issue had a way of looming much larger than in my present city congregation. I have learned that running away from problems never works. There is no substitute for facing an issue as soon as possible. Staying in close touch with people has saved me from shipwreck again and again. People have learned that they can talk to me, that I will listen, that I am adaptable, and that I will put people ahead of personal preferences. I am visible to the community, not tucked away in my home. As one member put it, "You can always find David. He's in his office at eight o'clock every morning; and except for when he's out calling, he's always accessible."

A word about the personal side of being a minister. As a single minister with a young child, I imagined I would be invited to people's homes a great deal. I was disappointed. A few families reached out, particularly the older members of the congregation, but most did not. Jonesville is a network of kith and kin, and people get together mainly as families. Consequently, I had to take the initiative. I invited practically the whole church to dinner through a series of Sunday evening dinner parties. But still, I found myself with many lonely evenings and weekends.

It became important for me to be real with my congregation. I did not hide my loneliness, and I did not hide my needs. I was myself, and most respected that. I did not hide the fact that one of the ways I spent my weekends was in brewing my own British-style ale. Nor did I hide the fact that I dated, often driving many miles for a date. Gradually, people accepted me as a real person and not just as a minister. So it was that, when I had been in Jonesville nearly two years, one of my church members called me to tell me of a singles meeting an hour away at which a Dale Carnegie talk was to be given. And there I met the woman who was to become my wife. When we married, so great was the tide of good feeling and the level of trust that my congregation allowed me to live fifty miles away and to commute each day, until the wearing mileage led us to move to a new church in New Orleans.

One thing I am not is a slave to work. Between us, we have four children. When I work, I work intensively. I get a lot done in a short space of time. But I also allow plenty of time for recreation with my family. I have discovered that only out of a rich personal life can quality ministry flow. I must experience life in all of its many dimensions and with all of its pressures if I am to relate to other people's lives.

The problem I faced in Jonesville for me symbolizes the problem my denomination as a whole is facing. We are a shrinking church, losing members at breakneck pace. No one seems to know what to do about it. But after my Jonesville experience, the answer seems obvious. Someone has said that the key to success is to find a need and fill it. If we are failing as a church, it is because we are not meeting people's needs. Quite simply, we are irrelevant to their lives. We are speaking a language, subscribing to a system of worship, and preaching in a manner that doesn't scratch where it itches. We are making policies at the national level that we are failing to articulate to our congregations. From the archaic liturgy of the local church to national General Assembly stands on international issues, people feel left out, their lives untouched by our ministry. We have a giant communications gap. But from experience, I know we can change. Our pews can become full once more, our policies vital.

■ 5 ■

The Small Church Experience

Wayne H. Keller

"Lord, I'm confused. With all of the talents and abilities you've given me, surely you have something more in mind for me than this? I can't imagine that you wouldn't want me as pastor of at least a three hundred- to four hundred-member congregation, one with enough power to impact the whole community for you. But, this congregation? It would be perfect for a recent seminary graduate, or a pastor about ready to retire. But me, Lord, me? Perhaps you've made a mistake."

"No, my child, I haven't made a mistake. I don't like making mistakes. I've called you, through these people, to serve this congregation of one hundred. Please remember, I, the Lord your God, sustain you and reward you, not on the basis of statistics but faithfulness. Doesn't that count with you? Aren't my presence and my promise enough to sustain you in the ministry to which I have called you?"

■ I ■

HAVE WE WHOM God has called to a small congregation ever had such a conversation with God? Have we wondered what we're doing serving a small congregation in our midlife, especially after having served a larger one? Have we faced the fear, the doubts, the anger that this is it, that probably the small church is our pastoral destiny?

WAYNE H. KELLER *is pastor of Trinity United Presbyterian Church in Sedro Woolley, Washington. He is author of the three-volume* Lectionary Worship Workbook, Cycle A-B-C, *published by C.S.S., Lima, Ohio.*

If we haven't thought about such questions, we need to, for at least two reasons. First, our biblical theology may confirm that God calls us, through a pastor-nominating committee, to a particular congregation. Our practical belief, however, may insist that our calling to a small congregation represents only the luck of the draw and the lack of proper recognition. Second, if our present ministry doesn't fulfill us now, maybe we never will experience fulfillment in ministry. If we sit around and wait for some larger congregation to call us, and depend for our self-worth on that next call, we may spend our entire ministry dissatisfied and miserable.

Those of us who serve small congregations represent the majority of pastors in America. Let us also recognize that we may never serve a larger one, let alone a large one. We can blame pastor-seeking committees who fail to recognize our assets. We can blame the denominational calling system. We can blame life for putting us in the wrong place at the wrong time. We can blame God for failing to fulfill our dreams and desires.

Blaming will do little for us or the people we serve. Yet we may continue to blame, and allow our anger to spill onto the people whom God has placed in our care. One pastor I know has served small congregations his entire ministry of thirty years. He tells of attending a small-church pastors' conference. Only he and one other pastor expressed satisfaction with their situation. The other clergy were frustrated, angry, and hostile, because they believed the denomination had failed to reward them by calling them to successively larger congregations.

Some church members contribute to this American success-oriented approach to ministry. When people in and out of the church ask about the size of my present congregation, they can only offer an embarrassed response when I tell them one hundred members, when they know that my previous congregation had four hundred.

Pastor-nominating committees often focus on the same issues: membership increases, budget increases, worship increases, salary increases. I know of a two thousand-member congregation that sought an interim pastor several years ago. For all practical purposes, the committee had decided whom it wanted, a person from another part of the country who had all the right credentials. At the same time, the chairman complained that the presbytery provided little help by not sending more names, more people to interview. The presbytery gave them at least one more person, someone whom they did interview, but who didn't measure up to their criteria. "We want the best, most qualified person in America," it was said during the interview, "and we will search the United States to find him." The pastor being interviewed was not their choice. He did not even receive his travel expenses. That hopeful pastor, who had no job at the time, needed a strong self-image not to allow the committee's attitude to discount or discredit him.

As the church, we can become so enamored of the American success story that we fail to look seriously at the Scriptures and church history. Bigness has infiltrated and infected us, so that our positive self-image depends on our getting called to the big congregations with the big budgets.

Barbara Wheeler, president of Auburn Theological Seminary, proposes that pastor-seeking committees, rather than focusing on whether candidates fulfill requirements, rules, and procedures, ask this single question: "What features of our polity, program, or theological position will you work hardest to change during your ministry?" This, she says, would serve as a sign that the local congregation knows it stands in constant need of reform. Few congregations may want to face that kind of future.

I know of a person who sought an interim pastorate in a large congregation. The committee let him know immediately what it didn't want. It didn't want him to deal with his personal struggle or pain. It didn't want to lose any members during his interim. And it didn't want him to remind the church how rich they were. He refused to accede. He did not receive the call. He did keep his integrity.

Pastors of small congregations need to begin, continue, and end with God's affirmation of them and their own identity and self-image as God's person. We begin with what we believe about ourselves. If our self-image comes from outside ourselves, through others' affirmations, we will face some painful and lonely times. As persons of faith, however, our self-image comes from a relationship with God. It comes from our willingness to live in the precious present moment. The pastor of the small congregation may need a stronger self-image than the pastor of a larger one. Are we willing to give up looking for our status in numbers, statistics, budgets, and large congregations?

I know of a pastor called to a four hundred-member congregation, a congregation rich in money, people, resources. From the beginning, he got invited to all the right places. The people wined and dined him. Groups from the community, from around the state, invited him to speak, to lead workshops. He became the congregation's conversation-piece in the beginning, and a community guru in the end. People from all over the area came for counseling. The congregation hummed. He became the talk of the town. That pastor loved the attention. He had become the big frog in the little pond. By the standards of success, he had it made.

But he worked himself into exhaustion. He enmeshed himself in the community. He spent less and less time with his wife. The more he did, the more people asked him to do. Because his self-image was founded on people's expectations and adulations, he kept producing. Then, the bubble burst. His burnout led to divorce. He was asked to resign. Most of his "friends" disappeared overnight. Shattered, exhausted, lonely, he resigned. He left the pastorate for several years, disillusioned, disenchanted, disgusted. Years passed. He decided to seek interim work to learn whether he wanted to return to the permanent pastorate. He decided to return, but had a hard time doing so. For two years he sought a permanent position. His only prayer during that search was, "Lord, make very clear to me where you want me to serve." He received thirty rejections without an interview. He received one acceptance, a call to a small congregation. He reports that God called him to the right place at the right time.

The struggle, bitter at times, taught him that success and attention are not criteria for ministry. They were not for Jesus. Whether our ministry is in small congregations or large, our self-image needs to center on God's calling, God's sustaining, God's fulfilling, God's purpose and plan for our lives, rather than criteria handed down by the American culture. Americans worship bigness and busyness. We have judged our self-worth and others' in terms of moving up in the system of bigness American style.

Intellectually we may believe our self-worth comes from God's affirmation and presence with us wherever we are, whatever we do. We need to integrate that belief emotionally. We need to study Paul's affirmations that, in whatever situation he found himself, he was satisfied, and "nothing in God's creation can separate us from the love of Christ." He urges us to give up our status-seeking through a doctrine of insatiable work that leaves us exhausted and hostile.

■ II ■

If we bring a Christ-centered self-image to the pastorate, we will discover and affirm the strengths of the small congregation.

Fewer People. Because the small church has fewer people, the pastor and congregation have a better chance of knowing each other in depth. That's not a foregone conclusion, unless the pastor and lay leaders care about every member, every visitor, every neighbor. This will require continuous reminding and creative organization, especially if the congregation has taken little initiative to develop and deepen its relationships previously.

People in small congregations—at least the leaders—assume that everyone knows everyone. Shy people never confront that assumption. Leaders may think everyone knows everyone, but they probably know only a little about each other through coffee hours, serving as church officers, or attending meetings.

Here are a couple of ideas that may contribute to a more intimate congregation. Divide the congregation into parishes, or cluster groups, of six to ten families. Assign a deacon to coordinate and an elder to assist. Suggest ways for the parish members to become acquainted—phone calls, notes and letters, planned and unplanned get-togethers, social action ministry. Support and encourage the church officers. Do not do their work. I have found that spending one hour per month with a combined meeting of the elders and deacons, after the deacons' meeting and before the elders' meeting, is sufficient to help the officers develop the program.

Such parishes will help people get to know one another. They also will help the elders take seriously their responsibility to minister to the people they received into membership. I use the parish structure for the every-member stewardship program. Families who do not return their pledge card on Stewardship Sunday receive a visit from their parish elder or deacon. About 95 percent of all pledge cards are turned in during the first week.

Caution. Give the officers and congregation time to integrate this ministry of the priesthood of all believers. If this is a new idea, some will approach it cautiously, especially if previous pastors have done it all themselves (which I call a McDonald's hamburger approach to ministry: "We do it all for you!").

Study Groups. To foster intimacy in the congregation establish study groups. Do this as quickly as possible, with groups of eight to fifteen, preferably meeting in homes. People can share the same congregation, even pew, for fifty years and never have an in-depth conversation about their faith. Samuel Miller of Harvard Divinity School once likened people in the church (I add, *as* the church) to marbles in a bag; they touch only at the outer edges. Yes, this can and does happen in small congregations as well as larger ones.

Caution. At the beginning of a new pastorate, I suggest the pastor do most of the teaching, unless the congregation has someone who has the education and ability to lead discussion groups. This gives people an opportunity to become familiar with the pastor's theology early in ministry. Group study and the attendant fellowship can bring people together and open them to new horizons, if the pastor gives them permission to disagree and challenge. Many congregations have never learned how to fight fairly. So they fight unfairly. New biblical awareness, with permission to express feelings, doubts, fears, and anger, opens new vistas of ministry, both within and beyond the local congregation. We need to keep reminding people that the church exists to enlighten and flavor the world of family, vocation, play, economics, and politics, the world for which Christ died.

In my own experience, for example, with both a large and a small congregation, I have developed the following study program: an eight-week seminar, an hour and a half each night, called "The Growing Edge: Dialogue with the Pastor," for those considering church membership, and open to anyone in the congregation or community who wants to explore the faith; weekly sermon discussion following worship; an overview of the Bible as drama, using Bernhard W. Anderson's *The Unfolding Drama of the Bible* as textbook, and William Barclay's *Introducing the Bible* as supplemental reading; Koinonia, small-group Bible studies meeting in homes twice a month for an hour and a half each evening (I study with one group on the first and third Sundays or Tuesdays, with the second group the second and fourth Sundays or Tuesdays; this has proved the most effective model—people will more often contract for twice a month than once a week); workshops, seminars, topical studies as the congregation requests.

Greater Depth. The small congregation provides an opportunity for growth in depth, especially by sharing feelings and needs, though again this is not guaranteed. Our society in general and the church in particular have done little to provide ways for us to be close. We have not learned well how to be angry in healthy ways and to forgive each other. In the large church, people can get angry and leave, and their absence may not cause much of an emotional or financial scar. In the small church, the loss of one angry member may lead to the loss of several. It is crucial for the pastor to model the handling of anger and to offer workshops on how to listen and how to resolve anger issues. If the pastor doesn't have such skills, community resources may exist.

Here's what I mean. Some members of the Presbyterian Church (U.S.A.) still hang on to their anger about the Angela Davis Legal Defense Fund gift. Some of our people never got beyond the three-line newspaper report. That event continues to affect the small congregation by having undermined trust in our leadership. Now that we have distanced ourselves from the event, we have an opportunity to interpret it and to find an acceptable model for future confrontations.

We can begin to discuss the Angela Davis Fund as one way that some Presbyterians chose to respond to Jesus' invitation to love our enemies. While many have criticized the decision, few critics have offered ways by which we, the church, can personalize our love for those we may think are out to do us in. Such a volatile subject, however, can create havoc in a small congregation, unless the pastor maintains a strong self-image, and, through the congregation's leaders, provides constructive ways for the people to talk and respond. The small church provides the forum for pastors to use every bit of skill, education, awareness, and insight they possess. Pastors need the wisdom of a serpent and the innocence of a dove. Pastors with any empathy and concern for people's wholeness will have a hard time not dealing with people in the raw. We need to remind ourselves that God calls us not to succeed but to remain faithful.

Pastoral Presence. The large congregation may call a pastor whose main responsibility is visitation. The small church has no such option. Either the pastor does the visiting or it doesn't get done.

During the rise of the human potential movement, some of us gave up pastoral visitation in favor of pastoral counseling. If we had special training, we received affirmation for our counseling abilities, and we stopped visiting people on their home turf. I've known pastors who even refused to visit homes and families in crises. If we neglect visiting our people, we are missing one of God's great opportunities for ministry. It's easy to get involved in community and denominational activities, workshops and seminars, clubs and service organizations, and to insist that's where real ministry lies, out there with the "important" people. Who gets neglected first? The people who can no longer "do" anything for us and the congregation—the elderly, the ill, the bereaved, the hurting. I'm not suggesting we ignore the wider community. As small-church pastors, however, we need to be selective and sometimes say no.

Some years ago, I served as chair of a presbytery committee on evangelism, which put me on the synod's committee as well. I became so involved in committee work that I had little time to spend with the local congregation. During that time, I did less evangelism through pastoral calling than at any other time. The congregation suffered from my absence, even though we were using the parish plan effectively.

If we spend time with our people, beyond merely shooting the breeze, we will discover several strengths. Members and nonmembers will come to trust us, and to share more and more of themselves and their particular concerns, needs, and friendship. With some, this will happen on the first visit. If we are willing to listen, especially to feelings underneath the words, we will discover that people will reveal their deepest hurts, which they may have buried for years. After getting to know an eighty-year-old in her home, during a social hour after worship one day, I recall her crying and saying, "I want to tell you this . . . something I have never said to anyone my whole life." That experience needs to become the norm, not the exception.

People will provide for us the teaching and preaching agenda of the church. If we listen at all, we will discover areas in their lives that need to experience the healing of the gospel. Give them the chance to raise questions, doubts, fears, and angers, and speak to those issues.

People will give us permission to preach the whole gospel and not merely our favorite segments of it. Of course, they won't always agree. The more they trust us, the more freedom they will give us to speak about issues of family, drugs, economics, and politics, as long as we identify our teaching with biblical theology.

■　　**III**　　■

There are further areas of *caution* to be alert to in the small church.

Fewer People. Although a potential strength, fewer people may become a burden, especially if some church members are interrelated. Offend one and you may offend several. "If I don't hear what I want, if you don't do what I want, I'll leave—and I'll take several with me," comes the threat, spoken or unspoken. One day an elder said to a pastor, "You have two choices around here: you can do what we tell you or you can leave." Deserted by his presbytery, he left; he still doesn't know what happened. Fewer people may also mean overwork by a few to keep the institution going, especially in older congregations. A few people have done all the jobs for years. Now they're too de-energized, exhausted, infirm.

Response. Keep administration simple. Visit both members and people in the neighborhood. The Jehovah's Witnesses and Mormons keep growing because someone spends time knocking on doors and inviting. My dad waited thirty years for someone to ask him to participate in the church's life.

Overwhelmed Secretary. Small congregations may have an overworked, underpaid secretary who does the work simply because of her (deliberate use of the pronoun) commitment. If this is allowed to happen, the congregation takes her for granted and expects a "free" secretary. I know of a secretary who was hired for 20 hours a week but who never worked less than 125 hours a month. Those kinds of hours and expectations are fair to no one. The congregation needs to know what's happening, and to respond where it can to lighten the burden.

If the congregation has no secretary, the pastor will do it all. That too is not fair to the pastor or congregation. The more we clergy do, the more people expect us to do. Unfortunately, maybe we get our affirmation by hearing people tell others how busy their pastor is. Maybe we like that image. But when the pastor becomes "the church," the people learn little about what their presence as the body of Christ means.

Response. Ask that the governing body find a part-time, even unpaid, secretary, if necessary, to do the detailed work of office administration. Make the job description specific. In addition, include the members in the work of the institution. For example, they can produce the church newsletter and directory. Spend time in worship and classes teaching the people ways to be the church in their homes, neighborhoods, and community organizations.

Fewer Programs. In this era when people choose a congregation for what they and their children can get, namely, all the benefits of Christianity but often with little or no thought about the demands of Christianity, many ignore the small church for the greener pastures of the larger congregation. Notice the methods we use to attract people to our congregation: "Come and hear our pastor; you'll love him (sometimes her). We have a great choir. We provide programs for all age groups. We are the friendliest church in town. Come and benefit from what we have to give you."

In his book *The Structures of Prejudice,* James Sellers says that we usually come at church participation and membership backward. Instead of telling people that "the kingdom has arrived in our church" (a danger when clergy get together to discuss how well things are going at their churches), Sellers suggests that our point of contact with the world outside the church be a point of conflict in the world. The point of conflict must be sin, the fact that we are alienated from God, each other, and our best self.

Response. In the small congregation, we have the opportunity to live out the message of alienation and reconciliation with each person individually. Refusal to do so will result in extreme discomfort for all. And the days will drag as we wait for another congregation to call us. In the small church, we have the best opportunity to involve every member in faithful worship attendance, ongoing Bible study, a specific job in the church, and prayer for the whole body of Christ.

Survival Only. The author of an article about the small church insists that the church of one hundred members "can almost run itself." About ten people, maybe less, can keep the institution humming.

Response. Keeping the local congregation humming is not the church's goal. The church exists for mission, for those outside of its membership as well as within. I'm not discounting the need for nurturing and educating the membership. But when the church focuses primarily on keeping its doors open, it often becomes self-centered and spends its energy on self-survival. The church is called to lose its life for Christ's sake in serving.

The Lord speaks once more:

"Now, do you understand? Do you see that I didn't make a mistake by calling you to this congregation? I have given you to these people because I love you and them. I have given you an opportunity to serve this part of my family. No, they won't always agree with you. They haven't always agreed with me. And please remember, you haven't always agreed with me either. I'm aware, better than you are, that my family, including you, argues, pouts, throws tantrums, gossips, blames, withdraws, apologizes, returns, and starts again. I've called you to be with these people, because I need someone with special skills, a loving heart, common sense, a solid relationship with my son, and a strong self-image, namely, my image in you. Please remember, my child, that your battles are mine, and that I've already won the victory. I'm calling you to faithful obedience in the precious present moment as my person, and I will never let you down."

"Thanks, Lord, thanks."

■ 6 ■

Today's American Gothic

Joanne D. Hines

OUR IMAGE of the small, rural church in America may look something like this. There's an old, plain church with a steeple in front. Seated inside on rows of old wooden pews are small groups of farm folk. They are dressed in overalls and gingham dresses, and scrubbed clean except for the mud on their boots. The congregation is sparse, scattered throughout the church in family groups. The church service is followed by a potluck on the front lawn of the church. It's a scenario that tugs at our heartstrings as we see the plain folk rooted in the land worship their God. The simplicity of life lived close to the land reminds us of our roots and the roots of America.

The towns are similar in name: Four Corners, Pike's Landing, Smithville (or anything ending in "ville"). There are towns named after the persons who founded them and towns describing a location: Watertown, Five Mile Creek, Crow's Landing. What these places have in common is what makes them rural. They are places where ranching and farming take place. They are in the country and not in the city.

But the face of the small, rural church across America is much more varied than this imaginary picture. It cannot be captured by any one place or church. The rural church has many facets and dimensions, many sizes and shapes. It is a constituency of many kinds of people and many life-styles. Although the definition of the rural church will change from place to place, the one thing we have in common is that we are in the country. That means the city is where you go to find traffic lights, traffic, "bigtime" entertainment, shopping centers, and a high crime rate.

JOANNE D. HINES *is pastor of Kelseyville Presbyterian Church in Kelseyville, California.*

The rural church is a member of the commonality of churches, city and country, that join the flow in the stream of Christianity. "There is a river whose streams make glad the city of God, the holy habitation of the Most High. God is in the midst of her, she shall not be moved" (Psalm 46:4-5). Ministry roots in the small rural church, exists, continues, and flourishes in these areas. The small church is itself a stream that flows into the mighty river of churches moving toward the kingdom of God. Streams both great and small contribute and have as their ending place that kingdom common to churches large and small, rural and cosmopolitan.

Ministry and mission have been carried on in many of our small towns for hundreds of years. God wants ministry here or it would not have survived the hardship of being isolated and small, nor experienced the joys that come from being isolated and small.

■   I   ■

Kelseyville Church ministers in a small, rural community in a coastal volcanic basin. A large lake forms one of the community's boundaries, a mountain range another. Surrounded by fields producing pears, walnuts, kiwi fruit, and grapes, it lies in farming country. The lake provides not only water for irrigation but recreation for tourists. This area is distinctive in many ways, yet similar to other rural communities.

Our congregation is distinctive in that it is a mixture of many folks. There are not only farmers but, because of the large retirement community here, people from many walks of life, mostly unrelated to agriculture. In addition, the area draws a variety of people to fill a variety of jobs, countywide. Gold mining and geothermal exploration in the mountains around the county bring people with experience and expertise in many occupations. In addition, the teacher, the artist, the author, the engineer, the laborer, the nurse, dentist, banker, and builder all sit next to each other in worship. There are the lifetimers, people born and brought up in this county, and there are those who have only recently moved here. Many have come from the city just to get away from the bright lights and back to the simple life.

While not all are farmers in this rural atmosphere, we all have strong ties to the land, which is a source of life for the county. Life revolves around the harvest, as much symbol as fact for the many who work the land. The County Fair, the Pear Blossom Festival, the 4-H barbecues, and the obvious changing of the seasons from blossom to fruit to bare tree remind us as we enter and leave this town of how much the crops represent a way of life and the lifeblood for our world.

The farmers are no longer just planters and rakers. They are educated business people. And they are just as apt to be women as men. No longer is it possible to make a successful living from the land without extensive education and expertise in everything from economics to insect sprays. Young people, graduated from high school, often move away from the county to find fame and fortune and higher education. They also tend to return later in life, because "small" and "rural" are, more and more, positive features in our complex world.

Churches such as this one have the disadvantages that a rural community can bring. But they also have joys that make people want to trade in their city life for a back-to-the-country life.

The stability of our church comes from its longtime families. This base is necessary to the rural church's survival because new families often do not stay long. Many people moving to the area find that, although they love the rural atmosphere and want to raise their children here, the economy is also depressed. Work is not plentiful. It is not easy to come into this type of community and make a living. People living in the country often find they must commute to the city to make a living and then return after a long drive in order to be able to live here.

The church serves as the stable part of life for many of these people. The fellowship, friendliness, and family character of the church are among its attractive assets. People are concerned about one another and try to help one another. The church is small enough for people to be aware of each other's problems, the church's problems, and community difficulties. They are able to respond personally, to minister to each other, and to be parents and grandparents to children in the congregation.

In the large church a person can perhaps hide. In the small church, everyone counts. Everyone contributes to the fellowship in some way. Anyone missing is noticed. Anonymity is not possible here. At the same time, it is good to feel needed and involved.

There are disadvantages to being a small, rural congregation. We do not have the resources of the city to turn to. We must survive on our own resources. We draw upon the congregation to accomplish everything from plumbing repairs to stewardship campaigns. We do everything from making the music to doing the evangelism. We are seldom able to hire church personnel to do "ministerial tasks." We learn to do them ourselves. Practical ministry runs the gamut from personal evangelism to leaky roof repair. Talents people didn't know they had are tapped. Our church has shown its talents in many ways. For a small community, we have a great interest in music, and our choir is excellent. We call upon those with culinary talent to host a Harvest Dinner for the whole community. We have rebuilt and refurbished our old social hall into a new hall for the church school and small group gatherings, and we have built a new social hall complex to accommodate our growing congregation. Heritage Hall reflects more than 115 years of ministry in this community, the work of countless people who are its local saints. Friendship Hall speaks to us of our future. The pride of accomplishment and the love of God make it worth the effort. We learn and make mistakes and grow together.

There is a strong family feeling in this church. Some people are related to each other, but most find that this fellowship really is the "family of God," with room for them. Like any family, it has its quarrels and differences, and its hierarchy. We love our children and take pride in recording their growing up among us. We celebrate our elderly and rely on them to represent a sense of history and stability in a rapidly changing world. Our children bring us a sense of hope for the future. Our older members know this hope is of historic value, because they have seen the church prevail through generations. They see the church struggle with a seemingly insurmountable problem and smile as they remember having faced a similar problem and lived through it in the past. The young people bring us new ideas; the older ones know where to turn off the water and gas in case of an emergency. Between the new and historic, the rest find comfort to gain perspective on what the church is all about.

Worship combines the old and the new. The buildings, pulpit, stained-glass windows, and sanctuary furnishings are almost all memorial gifts. They remind us of the saints who have gone before us. The service is a mixture: child and youth readers and children's sermons balanced against the old hymns and anthems and the creeds and confessions of the church of the ages. We are old and we are new, we step backward and we go forward, but we still flow toward the kingdom of God.

Because we are a family in the broadest sense, we have concern for all its parts. We, the members of all ages, are concerned over drug and alcohol abuse in the community. Even in our rural, unpolluted atmosphere, drugs and alcohol make their way into the culture. We are concerned because school and organizational activities cut into church and family time and our Sunday school and afterschool programs are not as full of children as we would like. We are concerned about the pressures and stresses of family life. In an area surrounded by nature and quiet, turmoil still manages to intrude. And we are concerned about the quality of life for our aging and elderly people. People who have grown up here and who love this countryside may be forced to leave because senior housing and health facilities are not adequate. The lack of facilities for our retired persons, 30 percent of the people, makes "gracious country living" difficult. The church tries to be a leader in making sure it is accessible to the handicapped and in assisting those with hearing and sight impairments. We try to minister to all ages and all needs, yet we cannot do enough because of insufficient time and resources.

This whole community is family also. It is still small enough that we can celebrate when a child is born and mourn when someone dies. Notices for funeral services are found first at the local post office because the paper is not published every day. You may see a birth announcement in the window of the local market before it reaches the statistics column of the paper.

Pastoral counseling is as likely to take place at the market or on the way to the post office as in a formal office setting. The minister and the people have a chance to get to know each other as people. The people meet at informal concerts and picnics, high school football games, and back-to-school nights as often as they meet at church.

This family spirit is alive too in the cooperation of other churches in the county. This cooperation is necessary to provide the many services that larger, urban churches can afford to provide on their own. The local food closet, shelter, emergency services, and community and individual disasters are handled by many of the churches. Worship services at the convalescent homes, hospital chaplaincy, radio ministry, and other services to the community require cooperative effort. In addition, there are cooperative Thanksgiving and Christmas Eve services and other common gatherings. There is little room for competition in a small town. It only serves to alienate one part of a family from another.

Our congregation is made up not just of Presbyterians but of a multitude of denominational choices: Christian Church, Catholic, Baptist, Congregational, Methodist. And because we are so far from other churches of our own denomination, we are not inclined to be rigidly denominational. Those who are on the board of the local church or who hold office in higher judicatories feel the ties. Many do not. For the person in the pew, the church often functions on an independent level.

■ II ■

The challenges to the small, rural church are many. One challenge is to be open to new people and new ideas. A church that has a family feeling sometimes is not open to letting others into the family. We have been blessed by that openness and an ability to welcome newcomers. But the challenge for this church is to be open to different types of people. In this agricultural area, we need to be aware of and accepting of cultural changes taking place because of the influx of Hispanic migrant workers into the community. They have long been present and accepted as a part of the community. With the new amnesty law and the Presbyterian mission to the Hispanic community, we must do more than just acknowledge their presence. We must be partners with them. This challenge has presented itself in peacemaking efforts and in a program for Hispanic women, the Amigas de Jesus. During off-seasons for harvesters, Hispanic women meet at the church to study, learn English, and enjoy fellowship. These women develop their talents, learn new skills, and share with us the privilege of serving God. A Hispanic Protestant church has developed from these small beginnings. This church is a shared ministry among many of the churches in the area.

Another challenge is our outreach to the farm and migrant workers in cooperation with the service agencies. Here we forget barriers of denomination, race, and creed. One such outreach, with the help of the Lion's Club, resulted in eye surgery for a Hispanic member of the community.

We are also needed when disaster strikes. Like many places, we seem to go from drought to floods. The church has assisted disaster crews in evacuating flood victims. We have set up three meals a day for days for weary crews needing a place to rest and eat a good meal before going back out on the lines. The disaster relief program started with a speaker addressing first the board of deacons and then the congregation. As a result we asked, "What can we do?" In times of disaster and emergency, the church pulls together from early morning to late night.

A further challenge is in the area of personal evangelism and mission. For the small church, it has often been the work of the pastor to speak the good news to the community on behalf of the church. The pastor does serve as public speaker, representative of the church on local boards, and public figurehead in areas of outreach and public service. But the real work is done by the people behind the scenes, those who do the committee work, give support to those in need, and often ask people to come to church with them. The church grows and reaches out when pastor and people work together.

The heart of mission for the small, rural church is another question. We cannot support large mission programs. We do not put on elaborate mission fairs. Mission in the small church is what happens when we respond to a common problem or empathize with a national disaster by sending whatever we can. Mission happens when a family is in distress and the local people gather around to help. Mission is serving, not just in church, but in the "shared commitment" relationship in the community. Everyone's help is needed, not just for the church, but for the 4-H, the PTA, the Little League, Hospice, the Food Cupboard, and other activities vital to the life and spiritual health of the community. The people in a small, rural community are busy, perhaps busier than they might be in a city.

The joy of living here is in the living, growing things around us. It is a joy to share not only in our own Sunday school growth, but in the public school's baccalaureate and graduation ceremonies. We cheer for our football teams on Saturday and worship together on Sundays.

Sometimes we find ourselves falling into a small town mentality: "we're not good enough, or big enough, or financially secure enough," and we do not have the programming and staffing capabilities of a large church. Or "what was good enough for Grandma is good enough for us." Such ideas often inhibit new ideas and ways of doing things. But the church is well educated, wise in commonsense values, and adventuresome enough to overcome much of this way of thinking. The stereotype of the small church as narrow-minded, uneducated, and backward does not hold true here. Although the wheels of acceptance of "cutting-edge theology" grind slowly, they probably do not grind any more slowly in the small church than in the larger one. "Small" does not mean underutilized, less well organized, or poorly done. Although we never think of ourselves as a corporation, we are aware of striving for excellence in all that we do. We would never want to use our size or our location to be less than God wants us to be.

■ 7 ■

Become a Part of the Lives of Your People

Benjamin E. Blumel

I AM NOW in my eleventh year as the pastor of two small churches in east central Ohio. All of my pastorates have been in small rural congregations, although prior to coming to my present pastorate I served in judicatory and ecumenical positions for eleven years. During those years, however, I maintained relationships with small congregations. My present pastorate is probably my last, because I plan to retire in a few years. I want to reflect on my ministry to the Carrollton United Presbyterian Church, which is in a small village.

Carrollton, population twenty-eight hundred, is the county seat of a county of about twenty-eight thousand residents. It is surrounded by farmland and smaller villages. Carrollton has a high percentage of older persons, because many people retire to Carrollton from the surrounding area. The county also has a high summer population because of the lakes to the west and the south. It is a conservative community, as evident in its politics and its resistance to change.

■ I ■

My ministry in Carrollton has been highly pastoral. There are two reasons for this. Pastoral concern has been a pattern

BENJAMIN E. BLUMEL *is pastor of Carrollton United Presbyterian Church in Carrollton, Ohio. He is editor of* Ministry in the Small Community, *the newsletter of the Presbyterian Town and Country Church Network, and of the* ATARC NEWS, *the newsletter of the Association of Town and Rural Congregations.*

throughout my entire ministry, and pastoral needs were what I faced most often during my first year in Carrollton.

I remember the advice of a minister I worked with while in seminary, "Become a part of the lives of your people." I still believe this was good advice. I am convinced that to carry out a pastorate in small congregations you must fulfill the pastoral role. This means visiting in homes, hospitals, and nursing homes, and ministering in times of serious illness, death, and family crises. It is fulfilled as you participate in the significant events of people's lives. Early in my ministry at Carrollton, two members of the congregation had terminal cancer, another had surgery for cancer. This congregation had and still has a high percentage of older persons. There have never been less than four members in their nineties. We also have had a large proportion of shut-in members.

The minister in small congregations must do more than simply fill a role. The minister of small congregations must become a friend. There is joy in this, but there is also pain, because you suffer the things your people suffer. When a member of the congregation dies, you lose more than a parishioner, you lose a friend. Fulfilling this pastoral role is time-consuming. Sometimes I feel I put too much of my time and energy into it, but it is what makes other ministry possible. When I arrived in my second pastorate, the congregation was deeply divided. I am convinced that by carefully making myself the pastor of the whole congregation I was able to get them to work together and to build bridges between the two groups. I expect that I will continue to accentuate my pastoral role as a minister, although I am aware that this priority is not shared by many of the ministers around me.

I have a theory about ministry that I call "money in the bank." You get money in the bank by caring for people in times of difficulty and need, and by being faithful in ministry. There are times when we then draw on this money in the bank: when we make mistakes, when we fail to be sensitive to some situation, or when we do or say something that others disagree with. As long as we have this money in the bank, we have the freedom to carry out our ministry in ways that we feel we ought to, but we must not overdraw our account.

I believe we must manage our pastoral responsibilities. One way that I have tried to make my pastoral work manageable is to keep a card file for each household. On the back of the card I write the month I last called in that household, and I place it six months forward. This helps me not to forget some people, and spaces my visiting. My wife, Nell, who is a nurse and has worked in clinic and public health situations, calls this a "tickler file," as such a device is generally known.

■ **II** ■

When I came to this church, I felt that the program of the church needed broadening. One of the first things we did was to form a choir, which had been absent for a number of years. We found a woman in the congregation who agreed to be the director and we started. Normally the choir has about twelve members, about a tenth of the membership. Around Easter the choir puts on a cantata. Then there are usually four to six additional persons singing. The choir has improved congregational singing, made it possible to discover musical talent we did not know we had, and improved the self-image of the congregation. One woman had said that when there were community events, we could never provide a choir like the other churches did. She had to change her concept of our church.

A second program started was for grade-school children. This meets after school on Fridays. It includes refreshments, study, singing, and recreation. In the last two years this group has practiced for and performed Christmas and Easter musicals. It has not only provided a ministry to this age group, but has enabled us to reach families with children who were not participating in our church. We will soon begin our eleventh year. Two years ago one of our members, who teaches fifth grade in the local elementary school, discovered that the majority of her pupils did not attend church or Sunday school anywhere. She invited them to come to youth club. When she did this again last year, it enlarged the group and put us in contact with a number of families with whom we had no previous contact. Over the years we have received members as the result of this youth program, and we expect to receive more. This development has been significant, since outreach has been one of our difficulties. Most of our members have not realized that there are a great number of unchurched families. Their friends tend to be members of our church or of some other church. One of our major challenges is to find additional ways to reach these unchurched people. This year we formed an Evangelism Committee and have had a Faith Discovery Weekend, a program developed by a seminary professor to help people think about how their own faith developed, who had a part in it, and then to see how they can share their faith. We are exploring other programs at the present time. To have a stable future the church needs to grow, not to become a large church, but larger than it is now.

The church building was built in 1886. It was severely damaged by fire in 1937 and was rebuilt. The fellowship hall in the basement was small, and was crowded for nearly any activity. The restrooms were inadequate. Two years ago an addition was built. The restrooms, boiler room, and kitchen were moved to the addition, making it possible to enlarge the fellowship hall, which thus became more usable and attractive. It would have been difficult to carry out some of our present activities two years ago. We are fortunate not to have an overly large building. The congregation fits well into it. We tried not to overbuild but to add adequate space. A neighboring church overbuilt when they added to their church several years ago and are saddled with a church facility too large for their needs and too expensive to maintain and heat.

■ III ■

Another ministry I have become involved in is a pastoral ministry in the county home. We had two members there, and in visiting them I found myself visiting others. Some of the residents now attend our church. One has become a member, and another will soon do so. They not only attend church but also participate in other activities.

As a minister I participate in community activities, ones that do not directly benefit the church. But I believe I should be involved in the community and am one of the few ministers here who participate to any extent. I am a member of Kiwanis and of the board of the Friendship Center, a local senior citizens agency, and recently became active in the Community Development group. I feel that it is important for a minister to have interests beyond the local church, both within the community and beyond. Some of my involvement is made possible by the length of my pastorate. I am not so much an outsider. While these activities in the community and beyond do not directly add to my ministry, they give me an opportunity to broaden my interests and lessen my sense of isolation. The isolation of small church ministers and town and country ministers has been written about and discussed extensively. The problem is compounded by limitations on what ministers in these churches can afford to do. There are things out there that we can get involved in, however, where our participation is welcomed and helpful and not a great expense.

By broadening my interests I avoid feeling hemmed in. I have served on synod groups and will begin to do so again this year. I have participated in the Ohio Council of Churches, and I am active in our synod and national town and country church organizations. I feel that it makes me more content and keeps me alive intellectually. But I am always aware of the danger of overextending myself.

One of the things that we need to do is broaden the activities of the Carrollton Church more than we have. Many years ago, the church had a group called the Young Adult Forum. Those who were a part of it are now in their sixties and seventies. We are currently making plans for a reunion of this group that will include persons who have joined the church since who are in the same age range. We hope not simply to get the group together but to stimulate the formation of a new young adult group, and perhaps a middle group. Currently we have a number of people in the twenty- to thirty-five-year range, but they are not as active as I might hope. Their stronger participation is needed if their children are going to be nurtured in the Christian faith, and if they are going to provide leadership for the church in the future. Our evangelism committee is making plans to try to develop some dialogue with persons in this age group to find what it is that they want from the church, and what would be meaningful to them.

■ IV ■

In the service for the ordination of elders, deacons, and ministers, the next-to-the-last question asks, "Will you seek to serve the people with energy, intelligence, imagination and love?" We need to do all these, but the one that we need most constantly to remind ourselves about is imagination. I have been here nearly eleven years. It is easy to develop a way of doing things and just coast on. Longer pastorates have the advantage of allowing a minister really to understand what is happening and to deal with problems. In short-term pastorates, ministers move away at just about the time they could be effective in problem areas, and thus the problems linger. The disadvantage of long-term pastoral leadership, however, is that there are not the fresh ideas a new pastor brings to the life of the congregation. With longer pastorates there must be personal and professional growth and the use of imagination and acceptance of new ideas. In the remaining four years I expect to be in Carrollton, I need to help the congregation broaden their program and try new things. I need to use my imagination and encourage them to use theirs, in order that together we can explore new kinds of ministry.

Early in my ministry I was invited to the Young Pastors Seminar that our church held at that time. People three years out of seminary were invited to a ten-day seminar three years in a row. This included lectures in theology, worship, and a variety of seminars. This was an important event in my ministry because I realized that I was not keeping as alive intellectually as I ought to have. I resolved never to let that happen again. Since that time I have engaged in serious graduate work while continuing in my ministry. Not everyone serving rural or small churches may need this, but I believe that disciplined study is important. If we need to serve with imagination, we also need to serve with intelligence. You cannot preach for eleven years to the same congregation if you are not renewing your understanding of the Scriptures and the world.

This church has not been heavily engaged in ministry beyond its walls, but it is involved to some extent. Members have been active in a project to renovate the county home both by contributing money and by participating in the group engaged in doing this. They have participated in the work of the ministerial association to provide food for families in need, as well as in the project to provide school clothes and school supplies for children in such families. They have contributed to the needs of a community north of us that was hit by a tornado two years ago. They have provided a meeting place for a 4-H group on a regular basis and for other groups on occasion.

I have tried to become a part of the lives of my people as I have served in this community. Some balance is needed in ministry. In a small rural congregation, a minister must be primarily person-oriented, rather than goal-oriented. We do have to have goals, structure, and vision in ministry, and we have to help the congregation have goals, structure, and vision. People here come first, however. I believe that as we develop relationships, we can better accomplish the rest.

■ 8 ■

In Search of Community
in the Community Church

James Crislip

WHEN NON-OREGONIANS think of Oregon, they
probably get a picture of forests and timber, snow-capped
peaks, rivers and lakes, rainy coasts, and populous cities. This
is one part of Oregon. Actually much of the state lies east of
the Cascade range and possesses a desertlike climate, with rain-
fall less than ten inches per year. North-central Oregon is characterized by bare, rolling hills, sagebrush, and grassland. The
summers exceed 100 degrees and winters head into subzero
snow and ice. Industry here means agriculture, limited by climate and shortage of water to wheat and barley farming. A
few folks are still in the cattle industry.

Moro, population three hundred, is the county seat of Sher-
man County. The county, covering more than fifteen hundred
square miles, has in the neighborhood of two thousand citizens,
widely scattered on large farms, and collected in several small
towns. As in most agricultural areas, the last decade has been
one of decline, recently made more severe by many of the same
factors affecting agriculture elsewhere. The population slowly
shrinks as jobs gradually disappear and farmers sell out. Other
small businesses falter, leaving behind empty buildings, board-
ed up, waiting for a fire or a bulldozer.

The people of the region are friendly and care for their
neighbors. Folks go out of their way to help each other. Whenever a call goes out for any kind of assistance, people volunteer

JAMES CRISLIP *is pastor of Community Presbyterian Church in Moro,
Oregon.*

whatever is needed. This is still a place where people often don't lock anything, and crime is virtually nonexistent. Moro is a near carbon copy of Lake Wobegon, right down to the Chatterbox Café, which is the Branding Iron here. There is no mail delivery, so most people make daily trips to the post office. It is a 100-mile round-trip to a supermarket or department store or any health professional. Hospital visitation takes at least a half day, or a full day if the patient is in Portland, a 240-mile round-trip.

The people of Moro fall into several distinct groups. There are large-scale farmers who did not expand at the wrong time and who are doing fine despite the economy. There are farmers who lease farmland and are heavily in debt and in varying degrees of difficulty. In each community there is a large segment of retired persons, and there is a distinctive group of younger families with one or both parents employed that could be characterized as middle class. A growing proportion of the population is unemployed and dependent on public assistance, and this group suffers the majority of problems, stemming from alcohol, drugs, and domestic abuse. This last segment the church struggles to reach.

■ I ■

Community Presbyterian Church is the only church in town, and that is both blessing and curse. The church attempts to serve a broad range of needs in a diverse population. In so doing, it sacrifices a strong denominational identity. The church just celebrated its centennial, involving the busiest flurry of activity in its history. The celebration became a rallying point for the church, an uplifting experience, and a wonderful education for me as pastor. I read nearly one hundred years of minutes from the church's governing body and from congregational meetings. I pored over the rolls and other records. I realized the church was doing as well or better now than ever, despite all the problems just outside its doors.

The theology of this church can probably be expressed by

telling about my first Sunday as pastor. I asked an elder to assist me in leading the service in the manner the congregation was used to. Prayers were addressed to Lord Jesus and not to God, and several people were audibly praying in Pentecostal fashion. The hymns I had chosen, like "All Creatures of Our God and King," were not, I was informed, of the usual character, and too difficult for the organist. The attendance on that day was fifteen, even though the church information form had boasted ninety-six active members. You can imagine the amount of time I spent in prayer the next week, ready to send out my dossier once more, before it was too late.

I stayed, and I'm glad I did, for the church and its activities have grown since I arrived. I started in small ways to get out and involved in the community. I joined the fire department. I took training to be an Emergency Medical Technician, and began working on the volunteer ambulance. In the fire department I became the medical officer and a lieutenant, secretary, and treasurer. I joined the Lions and am now serving my second year as the club's president. I started a Boy Scout troop and led it for two and a half years. I was appointed to the board of directors of the County Emergency Fund and brought Oregon Food Share (providing food to the hungry) to the county. I served on the Juvenile Services Commission, where my background as a school teacher served me well.

As I became involved in the life of the community, things picked up at the church. Average attendance on Sunday mornings is now near sixty. A variety of groups is functioning within the church family. A former seminary dean once said that taking on a church was like turning the *Queen Mary* around in dry dock. There would be lots of creaking and groaning, and it would be a slow process. I took his experienced word for it, and patience is winning out. When I arrived there was a session (the Presbyterian name for the elders' group) of six and a board of trustees of six, and neither had a clearly defined task, so there was conflict. The reorganized session of nine has absorbed the work of the trustees. Gradually I have come to know the personal lives of my parishioners, and have come to enjoy their acceptance.

■ II ■

With regard to theology, I was baffled upon first arriving in Moro. I was accustomed to the pluralism inherent in the Presbyterian way of doing things, but theologically this church and its leadership seemed to be of a different tradition completely. I thought that surely a church with a century of Presbyterian pastoral leadership would reflect that leadership. It turned out that the adult education in the church was handled for many years by a man who attended a conservative Baptist seminary in the 1930s, and—no surprise—the emphasis was on personal faith and commitment, and the flavor of adult studies was always devotional. At first I thought I should teach the adult classes, as the former teacher was now retired and traveling as a "film evangelist," taking Christian films to underprivileged churches.

For the first few Sundays I saw heads being scratched and noses crinkled. They had never experienced a theological or academic sort of study before, so I had to shift gears and meet them halfway. Their questions and observations ranged from "Where is the Garden of Eden?" to "Oh yes, the Jews—they killed Jesus." Eventually my wife took on the adults, launching into a six-year Methodist curriculum, a verse-by-verse study of the Bible, and the people have made it semidevotional and like it. I took on the junior high and high school age group, and found it more satisfying. I miss the adult teaching responsibility, but this church has no past model of the minister as teacher, though I will be teaching several short-term courses on a variety of subjects in the coming year.

Before coming to Moro I had served in a number of churches but had never encountered the kinds of thinking I found here. Yet I have come to understand these folks and to esteem them. There are even times, I find it strange to say, when only fundamentalism will do. When I strap on an airpack and crawl into a burning building, or when I am doing CPR in the ambulance, "O God, please help us" is the prayer of the moment. When we come out of the fire alive, and it is extinguished, or the person we seek to help on the ambulance is safely in the emergency room, "Thank you, God" seems to say it all. Many things about this kind of parish can get the pastor right down in the muck and grime of real life-and-death situations. This is rolled up shirt-sleeves ministry, and I confess that I love it. God has been more than gracious to me, packing every day full of practical experience.

■ **III** ■

My desire for the church to have a strong, clear identity still frustrates me, but that is surely my own shortcoming. I find the primary role of pastor to be dealing with those things that unite us as the body of Christ. To attempt to be exclusively denominational, or to point out people's denominational short-comings, would be destructive in these circumstances where so many religious backgrounds join together. Another role I have tried to develop is the pastor as mediator. There are extreme views on both sides of every political and social issue, and I try as best I can to help people understand the opposing view. The church allows me, as a Christian individual, the freedom to advocate a given point of view, but as pastor I have often found it necessary to foster understanding without placing myself firmly in one camp or the other. A pastor with a strong political or denominational stance would needlessly alienate a segment of the church. I see my task as building community in the Community Church, meeting people half-way on theological terms, and helping them to do so with each other.

Many people are associated with this church who will never join it because it is Presbyterian, while they continue to see themselves as Lutheran, Roman Catholic, Nazarene, or some other part of the family. This is in some ways frustrating to the pastor trying to serve and please everyone. Our polity requires at least one parent to be a member to present a child for baptism. That has caused some people to join reluctantly without really accepting the denominational ties of the church. When presented with the Book of Order, one longtime elder responded with, "Rules are made to be broken," or "We don't do it that way." Many feel the denomination is far too liberal for them. I use inclusive language, but members of the congregation are disturbed when the language of a familiar hymn is altered, or the words of a familiar Scripture passage or confession are changed. This presbytery insists on inclusive language in its proceedings, and this insistence raises the hackles of some of the parishioners. Some cling desperately to the inerrancy of Scripture and divine inspiration. Some will always be Pentecostal Presbyterians.

This is a church and a community on the edge of many things. Geographically, it is on the edge of a presbytery. Economically, the community and the church are on the edge of demise, due to the failing agricultural economy. Theologically, the church is on the edge of the denomination. Culturally, the community and the church are on the edge of present-day society. This is the blessing. Being on the edge constantly presents new and different challenges. There is never a shortage of work to be done when the hands are willing. The air is clean, the fishing is good, and the people are wonderful. There is no rush hour here. People take their time and do a lot of visiting. After a funeral, the minister stays behind with the funeral director, lowering the casket, enclosing it, shoveling some dirt. The pastor gets to take care of the church lawn and water the flowers. I built the new cross that tops the steeple. I fix the plumbing and electrical system and paint and clean. I visit the folks in their homes and at the hospital, probably my favorite part of the pastorate.

God has made me content with setting small goals and meeting them. The idealism felt in seminary has in time given way to the practical and the useful. I am learning to love old gospel hymns. I have acquired a taste for "Chicken on Sunday," and look for it at all the potlucks, which we enjoy anytime. I have learned to like phoning and reminding everyone of every meeting outside of Sunday worship. Phoning has proved to be not a frustration but another way to be in touch with the lives of the people.

I think it's fair to say that the community church like Community Church is not being addressed in the preparation of our clergy, even though it is these smaller types of pastorates that the seminary graduate usually encounters. I realize there is already too much material to impart in a seminary education. I want to challenge those preparing for ministry to consider the possibility of becoming a kind of "small church specialist" by taking more systematic theology for understanding, and concentrating especially on interpersonal skills. It is a task for the self-motivated and the self-reliant. The opportunities for diverse kinds of service are amazing. Some may find the tall steeple church grows less appealing when compared with the intimacy and human riches of the small rural pastorate. It has been so for me. God is good, and we are indeed blessed.

■ 9 ■

Change of Pace

Sandra L. Peirce

PERHAPS I SHOULD NEVER have uttered that fateful word "never." I know it rains every time I wash my car. But I don't really believe it's God who zaps me when I say "never." I admit there are lessons I need to learn here on earth, but I don't think every time I say, "No, I won't!" God says "Oh yes you will!" All I said was "I never want to live in that hick town." Not that I had ever lived in New York City. But San Francisco, where I was at the time, is action-packed, busy, lively, and interesting, and even my hometown in Illinois, in the greater Champaign-Urbana area, had a major university and a hundred thousand folks. Obviously God would not expect me to endure a cowboy town forty-five minutes from a shopping mall or movie theater, a town where a dummy hangs outside a saloon on Main Street and mean-looking guys hotshot around town in four-by-four vehicles complete with shotgun rack and shotgun.

I still understand the nonchalance with which I uttered the fateful word. Yet after six years of doing just what I said I'd never do, I'm even beginning to believe that God didn't arrange those years just to teach me a lesson. Nonetheless, there have been lessons. Perhaps they could have been learned in a big-city setting as well as in a rural town. Then again, perhaps not. I hate to have to eat my words.

■ I ■

The lessons have been important. The first was that it's okay for things to happen more slowly than I judge appropriate.

SANDRA L. PEIRCE *is co-pastor of El Dorado County Federated Church in Placerville, California.*

When you live in the country, time moves at a saunter more often than the gallop I assumed was necessary to accomplish the great ends of the church. Lots of folks who live here came to retire or to get away from the rat race they knew in the cities, and they refuse to be rushed. This causes untold frustration to high achievers who see a problem, envision a solution, and are ready to move straight to a satisfactory conclusion. For town folk, changes need to be mulled over, talked about, argued about, and the idea gotten used to before birth can occur. Coping techniques developed over a long time, based on a complicated history with many of the actors in the original drama still around, are not lightly given up. Even the sale of an old, worn-out piano takes a ton of negotiation and sensitivity for every dollar it's worth. "Such and such a family gave it and might have their feelings hurt." "We needed it when our Sunday school was so large. Why are there so few kids in Sunday school, anyhow? I know of a church where there are so many kids in church school that they could open their own school." "What if we need the piano later?" Accurate perceptions and challenging questions take time to sort out and address in a constructive way. A piano can be sold five years after the issue of its sale is brought up just as well as one month after, with feelings spared and minds willing to move ahead, even if the Sunday school attendance problem isn't quite worked out.

Friendships don't gallop into place, either. I was accustomed to moving into people's lives as quickly as I moved into their communities. In my previous experience, people had seemed willing, and none of us ever knew how long we might have before one or the other of us had to move on. In the country it is different. I remember being in the home of one of the young women of the congregation. She had invited the New Woman Minister to meet with a local group's executive committee as they planned programs for the next year. She was convinced they would like to meet me and hear my ideas. She was either naive, hopeful, or just plain mistaken. Of course I was pleased that they would like to meet me and hear my ideas, so I went prepared to present myself and the grand plans I thought would enlarge and enlighten. I was either naive, hopeful, just plain mistaken, or all three combined. My egotism exposed me to the pain of being politely listened to and not at all politely ignored. The plans for the following year did not include any of my good ideas. When my hostess hugged me good-bye that afternoon, she said, "Don't feel bad, Sandy. In ten years the women here will be your best friends." My reply was typical of my city assumptions: "I might not be here in ten years." In the six years since that embarrassing afternoon, the group has had at least one program on each of my proposals (I have even been the presenter for a few of them), and some of the women who were there are good friends indeed. It's okay for some things to happen more slowly than I deem appropriate.

■ II ■

The second lesson was that when you saunter you see the wildflowers instead of crushing them as you gallop faster and faster to get better and bigger and more. I've always liked the poem written by the old woman in reply to the question about what she would do differently if she had her life to live all over again. I remember the bits about eating fewer beans and more ice cream and stopping to smell the daisies. I've always liked the poem, but I haven't always followed its recommendations. It's easier here in the country, though, than it was in the city.

I'll be driving along some curve-laden stretch of road and come around a bend at the required twenty miles per hour to find a sun-drenched meadow by a little stream fairly dancing over the rocks that dot it and find myself compelled to stop and drink in the loveliness. One afternoon I asked a member of the congregation to be a Good Samaritan and transport me to a car repair appointment. As we reached the crest of a hill he said, "Pull over, quickly." Without knowing why, I responded to the urgency in his voice and pulled off the road and shut off the motor. "Look," was his first request. Looking like a beautiful picture from *National Geographic* were the Sierra

Nevada Mountains, their snow-capped peaks dazzling in the sunshine. "Let's sit here for one minute. I'll set the timer on my watch. Just one minute of appreciation." We sat there, absolutely silent before God's majestic grandeur in the mountains. Tears came to my eyes. The timer beeped. My friend laughed and said, "Wasn't that great. You're always hurrying around doing good things for everybody. You need to stop and realize how much God loves you that you've been given so much good to do." What a friend and what a cherished moment. When you saunter you can see the wildflowers instead of crushing them as you gallop faster and faster to get better and bigger and more.

The next lesson was that you can survive living in a fishbowl. Pastors of congregations in smaller communities are known, seen, evaluated by many people much of the time. I cannot go to the grocery store over my lunch hour to buy vegetables for supper without meeting someone I know. More likely I will meet many someones and endure comments like, "Well, I always knew ministers didn't live by bread alone," or field the questions like, "What time does my committee meet next week? I missed the last one." After an episode when one member wanted to know what I thought about the ordination of homosexual persons while I was trying to choose a solid eggplant for dinner, my daughters refused to accompany me to the store for weeks afterward. "You always have to stop and talk to everyone," was their complaint.

I did and I do. I wave at people I know, including my daughters' school friends—which they deem embarrassing at the best and deadly at the worst. I stop to talk to folks in the line at the movie theater (we finally got one, with four screens no less). I've been known to visit with some of the street people who have come to the church right on the Main Street for food or other assistance. I have found it an advantage to my ministry to live in a fishbowl. I hear and see things and know people and share life in a way that probably wouldn't happen if I tried to keep a low profile. If I can thrive in a fishbowl, anyone can survive in one.

Sandra L. Peirce

■ III ■

The final lesson—among the important ones—was that to be pastor with a congregation is hard but fulfilling work, but to be minister with the community is harder—and even more fulfilling. Because of the nature of the Presbyterian and Methodist understandings of the gospel and God's workings here on earth, and because of the personalities of the staff of our congregation, we are ministers with the community. Worship is central to the life of the congregation because you might not see many folks at any time other than on Sunday mornings. Since the local paper is published only three times a week, and then not everybody takes it or reads it, people who miss worship on Sunday are out of it until the next time. Mission is central to the life of the congregation out in the community. My list of involvements range from Retirement Community board member to high school guest speaker to Bioethics Study Task Force at the local hospital. There are few community organizations with which I have not met or for which I have not rendered one service or another. I have heard from members that they are pleased that "their" ministers are working in and for the community. Their support has made the community service possible.

The results of these contacts vary. Many of the weddings and funerals and much of the counseling I have performed have resulted from community work. I am even the unofficial minister for the theater bunch. When one of our most talented young actors died suddenly, the phone rang and a voice asked, "What can you help us do to celebrate his life?" It turned out his folks were Presbyterians. I officiated at the memorial service, visited at the mortuary, prayed with the family, and counseled close friends. To be pastor with a congregation is hard but fulfilling work. To be a minister with the community is harder and even more fulfilling.

Don't expect me ever to be foolish enough again to suggest there are places on earth where I would never live. I did that once and God proved me wrong. I don't like being wrong, but I am grateful for what I have learned. I still wash my car from time to time, knowing that it will immediately bring rain. So I guess I'm not surprised that I still say "Never!" about other aspects of ministry and then feel the cosmic zap once more. I should never have uttered those fateful words.

▪ 10 ▪

Ministry in
Three-Quarter Time

Ellsworth E. Jackson

LET ME INTRODUCE you to Marksboro Presbyterian Church in the village of Marksboro, New Jersey. It's a congregation of some sixty-five folk. The church building sits on a small parcel of land right at the edge of Route 94, a much-traveled highway and a favorite with eighteen-wheeler trucks, which runs from New Jersey into New York state.

The church is the only one in this village of some thirty homes, a general store, video store, bike and motorcycle shop, tire and pool supplies business, lawyer's office, and Cappy Reidel's place full of old farm machinery, much of it rusting away in his woods. Cappy is a Godsend to the few local farmers left because he has parts and the know-how to keep their tractors and other equipment running. Cappy is a good friend to the church inasmuch as he grants us permission to park on the edge of his land. The church sits on a postage stamp bit of land—there's barely enough room for fifteen cars.

Frelinghuysen is the name of the township of which Marksboro is a small part. It's a township of two thousand people in the rolling lush land of northern New Jersey. There's a school, a Methodist church, a post office, a dwindling number of farms and homes. Along with the township, Marksboro Church lies close to the Delaware River and the Appalachian Trail. The river, mountains, and trail divide New Jersey from Pennsylvania.

Marksboro takes its name from Mark Thompson, who came into the area in the early 1700s and developed the area and

---

ELLSWORTH E. JACKSON *is pastor of Marksboro Presbyterian Church in Marksboro, New Jersey.*

gave his name to the village. He lies buried in the old graveyard lying just behind the church building.

Marksboro Church belongs to the presbytery of Newton. The church began in the early 1800s. The present white frame building with bright red front doors is a replacement for the original building, which was struck by lightning in 1943 and burned to the ground. Members tell of hearing the news while they were busy milking their cows. "We dropped our pails and rushed up to the church to rescue what we could, the communion silver and pulpit Bible." Soon they banded together to rebuild. It took them a few years of holding supper after supper and benefit after benefit, but they finally accomplished their goal, and the wee church by the side of Highway 94 stands as a testimony today to their love of the Eternal. They did all of this without any assistance from the presbytery.

I speak of the church as being part of the village of Marksboro. However, there seems to be little contact or even friendliness among the people. One old-timer laments that whereas once upon a time she knew and was able to speak with her neighbors, now she knows hardly anyone.

Within a half-mile of the church is Genesis Farm, an expression of a community of Dominican sisters. Here is an exciting use of land, once an old farm. Under the sisters, especially Sister Miriam, the spirit behind it all, this farm is a place for new experiments in organic gardening, learning how to bake your own bread, and encouraging a more gentle ecological ethic. Marksboro congregation and Genesis have a fine relationship. Church members have helped the new community garden idea to get off the ground. Shares in the community garden were offered, whereby individuals and families could pay to receive organically grown vegetables and fruits for their own tables. People have volunteered time and energy to help care for and weed the garden.

Let me invite you inside Marksboro Presbyterian Church. The sanctuary is a gem of a room in its simplicity. There is a central pulpit with its Bible in the center on a raised platform. Behind the pulpit are the traditional chairs—three of them—with red seats. Up front on the floor is the Holy Table with two candlesticks and two offering plates. Seasonal liturgical hangings cover pulpit and table. One homemade colorful banner decks one wall with the words "Multiply thy gift!" The windows have full, tapered lines and are of clear glass so you can see the sky from the comfortable wooden pews (no cushions). The room plus the wee balcony can seat about one hundred people. On an average Sunday you will see about thirty folk present.

Topping the building is a small belfry. Inside this belfry is a small bell that belonged to a local steam engine when once upon a time the railroad ran from here to New York City, about an hour and a half away. Christy and Shannon and sometimes Nathan take turns pulling the rope that rings the bell for Sunday celebrations and other special occasions.

Downstairs you will find a room full of tables and chairs and an adequate kitchen. This multipurpose room serves as a place for Sunday school, youth group, committee meetings, various suppers, and the twice yearly rummage sales. The unisex toilet is in the back corner.

■ I ■

Naturally the focus of this Christian company is the Sunday celebrations. On any given Sunday you will find Marion Vitale at the electric organ and directing the choir. Marion gives her services freely as did her mother, Gertrude, before her. Members take their turns each Sunday welcoming one another and the occasional visitor with a warm greeting at the door. The weekly bulletin with the order of worship and any announcements for the week is prepared by Millie, a nimble seventy-one-year-old. One of the wonderful aspects of this small church is the way the various members of the congregation take up the various tasks. Truly, this fellowship expresses the biblical understanding of the priesthood of all believers. There's Florence and Herman. Now retired from the farm, they clean the church building when needed and cut the lawn around the building. Myron, Rita, and Estella cook the food for the dinners the church holds during the year. Rita and Frankie teach and direct the Sunday school of some eight to ten youngsters.

Estella spends many hours as the treasurer and youth group leader.

The congregation has an adventuresome and flexible quality that makes for the possibility of experimentation. When I came I learned that they had brought in clowns from a neighboring Presbyterian church. These clowns were to lead a special Sunday celebration. I suggested that this time we might, quite simply, be our own clowns and design a celebration of thanksgiving to the One who loves clowns. The elders said fine, let's do it. Of course there was some fear and trembling in the process. Many got into it. Some were skeptical and didn't dress up, but they came anyway. Members in their seventies as well as the younger set created all sorts of fascinating outfits. People experienced themselves in fresh and funny ways. It was such a joyous and fun time "playing before the Lord" that we did it a second time this year.

The people here are ready for anything, it seems. Recently I was sick. On Saturday evening I called Helen and Tom. I asked if they would be willing, even on such short notice, to lead the Sunday celebration in my absence. Even though Helen is a nervous elder, she agreed. I learned after that Sunday how well it all went, how Helen got other members to do the various parts in the service and how she used the sermon time to get people to share their faith. And with much nervousness, Helen led off!

■ II ■

It's been my pleasure for much of my ministry, which stretches back to 1950, the year I was ordained in my father's church in Germantown, Philadelphia, to have been in large congregations: one in Scotland at St. Mary's Church of Scotland parish outside of Edinburgh, in the First Presbyterian Church of Pittsburgh, and as senior minister for ten delightful years of the center-city First and Central Presbyterian Church of Wilmington, Delaware. I learned and grew in wonderful ways in each of these one- to two-thousand-member congregations. I was blessed with ministerial associates and with a personal secretary in addition to a church secretary. These were tremendous experiences working with men and women in busy, active situations. And here I am at the tender age of sixty-two about to be called as minister (I've been the stated supply minister, a Presbyterian term for a temporary) to a congregation in an out-of-the-way, small, rural fellowship of Christ's folk. It is ministry in three-quarter time. What's that, you ask? It's simply that I am part time, about thirty hours weekly. Presbytery designates my call as "three-quarter-time, not full time." So here I am, already partially retired, with time on my hands each week to do as I please.

A member of a large congregation in New York and president of a bank recently got to talking with a fellow minister of my acquaintance. As it happened, the elder-banker learned of my situation and asked my friend, "What's a minister with his background and ability doing in a small parish like Marksboro?" A good question. An American question. We who have been educated to think and work toward the large, big, and busy find it difficult to understand or even appreciate the small. I've had to deal with this because as a good American boy I've been so conditioned to despise the small, to think of the "small" as insignificant, not worth your time. And here I am, gladly embracing a small church in the rural setting of New Jersey. No doubt my conversion to loving the small has something to do with what happened to me in 1975. Then it was that my divorce happened, a painful and tremendous shock. Then it was that I experienced burnout as a man and as a minister. After three years as minister of a wonderful small, interracial Presbyterian church in the Throggs Neck area of New York City, I experienced the need for a sabbatical, a breather.

I gave myself an open-ended block of time just to breathe, to do nothing. I cashed in on the life insurance policy I had been paying for since my seminary days at Princeton. In short I used the money, about seventeen thousand dollars, to insure my life, my regeneration! Much of the period from 1975 to 1985 was spent living very simply and very leisurely. By the Spirit I was led to hitchhike the U.S. and Indonesia, especially Bali. I was introduced to beautiful people everywhere—people in small communities and small congregations of every denomination. Thereafter I was gifted a new Ford van and a stipend of two hundred dollars a month from my boyhood congregation in Philadelphia to travel with the Spirit all over America. I lived out of the van. "Black Moriah" was her name. To live in a campground in Big Pine Key, Florida, one entire winter. To be with the inhabitants of that campground as a friend and counselor. To support myself by working as the buffet steward in a fancy restaurant nearby. To learn to live with very little. To add a great dash of simplicity to my life and faith. I see this self-chosen way of living out ministry as a profound way the Creator Spirit had of humbling me for my next work in a standard-brand parish.

■ III ■

So here I am in the village Presbyterian church of Marksboro. And I am delighted so to be. Each week usually finds me over in the village and the township. I say I go "over" because there is no manse. So I live about an hour's driving time away in the Pocono Mountains of Pennsylvania, on an old farm my parents bought in 1949. It has been passed on to my sister and brothers and me.

This old farm with its woods and open fields lined with stone walls laid down by farmers here over a hundred years ago is not only my home but also part of the ministry of Marksboro Church. I see it as a refuge, a retreat space for individuals and clusters of folk from the congregation. There's a small cabin that has been my home since 1976. It has a potbelly stove and a sleeping loft, a small library, and an easy chair. Now it is a personal retreat space. The cabin makes it possible for an individual or couple to come here and get in touch with their own creative and divine nature. The trees, stone walls, and silence become the teacher. I know, because "it" has all been my teacher, the deer and the birds and the chipmunks, too. And the several outhouses, and the lively spring just down the way, which gives us our water, free, gratis, and for nothing. All you have to do is take a pail or cup, walk down, and lift the door, and you receive the most delicious water.

Recently I invited the church to come for a day. You bring the food, I said to them, and I will supply drinks and dessert. Twenty-seven came for a delightful time together. During the break from the summer rain, we played croquet and horseshoes, while some walked to the pond and others into the woods to pick the wild huckleberries. I have had the Sunday school youngsters and their teachers and the youth group, parents, and leaders up to tent and camp out for a night or two, and that's the way the church is growing.

Wednesday is the day apart from Sunday when I am regularly at the church. On Wednesday I am available for conversation and counseling. Often I schedule a half hour for reading aloud. This is announced on Sundays and a few come. Lately I've been reading stories of Native Americans and their various ways and spiritual worldviews. The elders okayed my using my study leave to study Native American peoples. Sometimes the time before 11:30 A.M. is given over to sharing our dreams or to plain conversation. At 11:30 each Wednesday we light the candles on the Table and, gathering around the Table, we fall silent. We observe a half hour silent meditation. We have anywhere from two to eight sharing in this vital time. At the finish there's a moment for sharing or questions. Then we hold hands and sing "Kum By Ya" or pray the Lord's Prayer together. Silent meditation sounds more like Quaker practice or even Buddhism than a way for Presbyterians. However, strange as it sounds to some in the church and community, it is a vital happening each week.

Often on Wednesday evenings we hold Bible study and time for prayer. I lead these times, but everyone who comes is invited to read aloud the passage and to share doubts and questions. We have as many as ten on these occasions. Recently for Lent we showed the Presbyterian video on the arms race and how it affects people of faith. Only a few members came, but it did attract some Unitarians and other concerned folk in the area. Marksboro Church is a recognized Peace Congregation and there is an active, if small, company of folk involved.

On the third Tuesday of each month is the Joyful Living Luncheon. We meet at noon. Senior residents in the church and community are the core group. Each person pays two dollars for the church-prepared meal. Usually Estella prepares the food and Shirley serves. We remember birthdays and wedding anniversaries with singing. There's grand fellowship and conversation about the tables. On a good Tuesday we will have over thirty diners. Last month Norma, an elder, brought a beautiful afghan she had crocheted. This was raffled off (don't tell presbytery) with everyone putting in a dollar. Helen won it this time. The money goes into the Ladies Aid Fund for local mission.

Marksboro Church is not only a small congregation. It's also a mission of the presbytery. For most of its history it has had a membership below a hundred. Moreover, it has been served by seminary students and a retired minister for a number of years. For over twelve years it was yoked with nearby Stillwater Presbyterian Church. One minister served both congregations, with each church maintaining its own elders, Sunday school, and worship. Since Stillwater Church has a manse, that's where the minister lived. In recent times the presbytery has taken special interest in Marksboro, reflected in the executive presbyter giving a considerable amount of his time plus a revitalization grant from the presbytery in the amount of twelve thousand dollars annually. With this added money the position of the minister was upgraded from half time to three-quarter time. Even though there are three other Presbyterian congregations within five miles of Marksboro, it was thought that, given the breaking up of farm land into two- to three-acre lots for new homes, Marksboro Church should get ready to receive the new families moving in from urban New Jersey and New York City. Marksboro with the surrounding area is now considered a major bedroom community for New York City.

I have been at Marksboro for two years. During this time there has been no great rush of new folk into the church. The evangelism committee made a special visitation into the village itself as well as going to the homes of the new folk. To date it would appear that this effort has made little if any difference. A few have visited, but no one has continued. Some say this is due to our tiny setting and that young families with children are put off by our lack of facilities. Others suggest that since Marksboro is like an extended family with everyone knowing everyone it's difficult for new folk to "get in." I hear all of this and I suppose there is a grain of truth in it, but I suspect the reason for the uninterest on the part of the new, urban neighbors lies elsewhere. The shift itself from an urban to a country setting raises more questions and dis-ease than people realize. In the city things are hopping; there's plenty to do. There are more people and there's a lot of noise. Here in the country, with the quiet and the open spaces, city folk begin to go bonkers. "Nothing's happening," they say. Then there is the farmer out there early in the morning and into the dark running his tractor, baling his hay, and spreading his manure, and the city person who has paid possibly $200,000 for his choice bit of rural land begins to wonder.

In addition to giving the church the revitalization grant (Marksboro chose to reduce this to ten thousand dollars this year), presbytery has encouraged it to purchase five acres of farmland at the other end of the village. The plan calls for the church to buy this land for sixty thousand dollars and then with loans from presbytery and synod to erect a fellowship hall, new kitchen, pastor's study, bathrooms, and increased space for parking. Marksboro people have voted to go forward with this plan, but since that vote was taken over two years ago, there are some folk who are now questioning the whole idea. I confess to sharing the doubt. What with our neighboring fellow Presbyterians experiencing little or no growth, and this with larger memberships and facilities than ours, one wonders whether the idea of enlarging Marksboro is not coming out of the older, dominant thinking in society as well as in church that bigger is better.

Furthermore, the issue of church or religious group growth has to involve the larger picture. Not only the picture of year-by-year membership loss in our own Presbyterian Church (U.S.A.), but the changing spiritual interests of people everywhere. One finds folk interested in their spiritual life, but not necessarily drawn to the expression of it in the organized congregation. So for a church like Marksboro, and for others as well, we are in a brand-new missionary situation.

98

■ IV ■

Schumacher's thesis that "small is beautiful" encourages us, the West in particular, to reduce our economic sights, to think and design small. His thesis has special value for us in religion. We who more often than not have been allied with the culture's dominant ethos are being asked to consider that "small is beautiful." But that's easier written about than taken on as a new understanding. Church folk are part of the society that preaches on every level—TV, magazines, radio, and film—that bigger is better, consume, consume, so the U.S. can continue to have the highest standard of living on the globe.

Small is beautiful, but it's also painful. Such an understanding calls for a profound change in our deeps. Herein is perhaps the particular vocation of the small congregation. Perhaps in our smallness—in numbers, that is—we have a special opportunity to be the people of God. The base communities of the church in Central and Latin America are small and for the most part led by the members themselves, with the priest coming by now and again. In their wee-ness is their strength and power to proclaim the good news. With little to lose, except their own precious lives, they are enabled in their smallness and their poverty to critique the economic, political, and religious structures where they live.

I see Marksboro congregation doing well in mutual ministry and care of its own membership. People pray for one another. They visit one another in the hospital and they deliver a basket of fruit or a spray of flowers when they come home. This is wonderful and part of bearing one another's burdens. However, there is more growing to come in us, me too, before we can address the issues of homelessness, hunger, AIDS, and the economic and political structures in America feeding it all and letting it be. When we begin to do this part of mission, we may grow even smaller.

Gladys Vough died the other day. She was eighty and the kind of person often referred to as a "pillar of the church." She was born in the area and lived in the village. At five she was milking the cows on her parents' farm. When the original church burned down, it was she who rallied the members and helped to raise the funds to rebuild. Every Sunday she was present. She gave generously of her time, energy, and money. The church turned out to celebrate her life. Now she is gone. I ask myself who will come to take her place? How will the congregation she loved reach out with the love and good news of God now? Her son Jim, one of several farmers in the church, has put the farm up for sale. He plans to move away. So it goes in Marksboro just now. Len and Bea have just retired from operating a motel in another town. They have moved into the area. They have moved next to Em and Dot, both elders. Em and Dot invited Len and Bea to Marksboro. Len and Bea have just joined, bringing their letter of transfer from a sister Presbyterian church. They are active and present every Sunday. Gladys can't be replaced, but the Creator Spirit has sent new life in Len and Bea. Praise be! So it goes with the people of God in the village of Marksboro.

■ 11 ■

Loving and Not Loving the Small Church

Thomas O. Elson

WHY DO YOU SPEND so much time with so few people? This question first made its impression upon me as a child when my missionary parents were asked by church people why they would go to small tribal groups to translate the Bible. In response they pointed out that in the U.S. pastors spend years pastoring small churches, so why not do the same in mission work? From them I learned a lesson that has had a deep influence on my own ministry as a pastor: numbers are not the main reason for ministry. The lives of particular people are more important, and the gospel message is essential for small groups as well as large, in any country on the globe.

Yet as I have pastored a small church, I have found the question persists. Is it really okay to spend years pastoring in a small church? Or is this some kind of excuse for lack of ability, motivation, or vision? It may be acceptable to be called to pastor a small congregation, but it is widely assumed that if ministry really takes place the congregation will grow. When growth does not occur, can such a ministry still be considered right, or is something wrong? Are those relatively few people to whom you minister worth it? The question persists.

This question becomes more personal when asked from the perspective of the pastor. Am I okay if I stay and minister in a small congregation, which may not have grown as I had hoped? Is there something wrong with me that the church has not grown, or is there something wrong with my commitment

THOMAS O. ELSON *is pastor of First Presbyterian Church in Lindsay, California.*

to the Lord, or is there something wrong with my leadership, or with my motivation, or my ability to minister? These questions face the person who has decided to remain in the smaller church for an extended time. They are nagging, ruthless questions and they require clear answers to continue in ministry where one is rather than look for a better, bigger, or brighter position.

A psychologist friend helped me see success in ministry from another angle. He had been seeing some clients for five and six years. At first, he said, this felt like failure. After wrestling with this feeling, he came to redefine his success. There are times when success means keeping a person alive psychologically, and out of an institution, or physically, by keeping them from committing suicide. Success in the small church may sometimes mean simply survival, even though the deeper desire is to help the congregation maintain a vital witness in its community.

If ministry in a small congregation is not only okay but essential, how is such ministry to be exegeted? With Scripture, my goal is to let the text speak for itself. Then I take the text's "self-word" and engage it in the present century and culture, so that it speaks once again. The exegesis of small church ministry is similar. One must look at the text (the congregation) and the context (the history, the ages, the backgrounds, the interests and needs) to see what has been written on these faces and in these hearts, and then let this word speak for itself. The pastor is one who helps engage the word of the small church with the words of the world. The small church undoubtedly had a vital ministry long before the current pastor came. Pastors do not impose an agenda upon a congregation, but seek to discover God's agenda already written in their lives and upon their hearts.

For this ministry, the exegesis of the small church, to happen, three related factors must interact: the exegete, the Word of God, and the congregation. To what extent these factors are unique to the small church I cannot say. I do know that my awareness of them came from my experience in the small church, and that because of this experience I was able to articulate them for my daily work.

■ I ■

The parish exegete must know who he or she is. The better I know who I am, what I believe, what I do not believe, when I tend to become angry, what brings me joy, the better parish exegete I will be. The more we are able to keep our prejudices and presuppositions in perspective, our tapes from the past and our fears of the future, the clearer we are able to see the needs and desires of the congregation and what we can do to help meet them. People in the small church quickly size up the pastor. If the pastor's view of herself or himself is significantly different from the people's view, a lack of integrity will be felt and trust will be more difficult to develop.

So who are we, who am I? Is this a question we dare to ask, and dare to answer? I have discovered that my life as a pastor causes me to reflect more on who I am than on strategy about the church. I have discovered interesting and sometimes disturbing things about myself. I often live more in the future, with its dreams and possibilities, and in the past with its unresolved pain and unmet goals, than in the present. I am often my own worst enemy, fudging on important preparation time, overscheduling program time, saying yes when no would be healthier, and no when an enthusiastic yes would be more wholesome. I am so intimately tied to this calling that I take most criticism very personally and most joy tentatively. I accept who I am on the Myers-Briggs personality inventory, but hold at arm's length who I am as seen on the pages of Scripture. I am at once a frightened little boy attempting to be responsive to God and the ministry to which I have been called, and a stubborn, strong-willed man who will do what he thinks necessary for ministry to take place according to his gifts, talents, and desires.

We must know ourselves as products of our own culture, yet also, more significantly, as products of God's creation. This self-discovery places us face-to-face with our society, our culture, our history, but also with God's analysis of us as seen on the pages of Scripture. In this ministry we come to know ourselves not only psychologically but theologically. It is this theological perspective—made "little less than God" and pronounced "very good"—combined with the view that "all have sinned and fall short of the glory of God" with which we must grapple. We all need to hear the word of grace from God, which grounds our humanity in the humility of God. It is from the perspective of the cross that we derive our theological self-awareness. From the Easter message we realize that "if anyone is in Christ, that person is a new creation" (2 Cor. 5:17). It is this theological perspective that grounds our psychological perspective in reality and enables us to minister a word of grace to God's people.

Another important reason we must know ourselves is that low-grade depression seems commonplace among pastors of small churches. The hope of a "high" calling gives way to the weekly routine. Seminary education and academic challenge give way to the desire for devotional simplicity or emotional fervor. The larger church background from which most pastors come must be recycled into the small church that most parishes are. The activity of the crowded classroom or noisy street gives way to the quiet of the pastor's office disturbed by an occasional knock on the door or ring of the phone. The thrill of seeing people change is modified by the realization of the need for change in oneself. These are all adjustments that can cause depression in the solo pastor who serves the small church. The better we know ourselves, the better able we are to deal with these realities which press for adjustment in our lives.

When we know ourselves, we are freer to listen to others tell about themselves and to enable them to discover their uniqueness and the special place they have in the body of Christ. Ministry in a small church is very personal. The better we know ourselves, the more we can give to and receive from others.

A pastor in a small church must know who he or she is, so as not to leave clutter in the way of what God might want to do in and through them. We must be able to hear our own heartbeat, so that we can also hear the heartbeat of the congregation, and sense where God is taking us together. One positive aspect of our narcissistic culture is coming to know ourselves as unique persons, and valuing the uniqueness of others.

■ II ■

The parish exegete must also know the Word of God. The Word of God stands over the exegete and between the exegete and the congregation. So the Word of God must be heard and listened to, known, digested, thought through, understood. Here we meet the men and women who have stood where we now stand, who have experienced what we now are experiencing, who have erred where we now err, who have been forgiven even as we need forgiving. Here we see the cycles in congregational life played centuries earlier by the people of God old and new.

We must know the Word because we are the public proclaimers of that Word. If we use passages of Scripture, whether comforting or challenging, merely to say what we want to say, we are being fair neither to the text nor the people who come to hear a word from God's Word. If a relevant word is to be spoken, then the biblical Word must be known. We dare to stand and speak not on our our own behalf, but on behalf of the living God. To do so with integrity we must know God's Word.

The parish exegete has been given one of the greatest privileges of all time, the call to study and expound the Word of God. In our role of preaching and teaching, we must hold sacred the time necessary to prepare adequately. If it is true we have been called to preach, then it is equally true we have been called to prepare. Much of this preparation is the hard but rewarding work of biblical exegesis. When preparation is given its full respect by pastor and people, preaching is given its fullest hearing. Because I believe this, it was a deep shock to me when the following two incidents occurred.

An elder came to speak with me one day. He was an old-timer who had made a significant contribution to the church over the years. We talked about a variety of concerns and then he turned to my preaching. His criticism, meant for my benefit, was that the sermons were too much like Sunday school lessons. They weren't bad, the content was good, the organization was acceptable, but they were too much like Sunday school lessons, too simple. Years later I still feel the sting of this comment. At the time the pit in my stomach stayed for several days.

The very next week another elder, again an old-timer, came to see me. She came to speak about my preaching. Again she came to help, since the people who spoke with her did not plan to give me this information themselves. Her concern was that my sermons were too intellectual. They were going over people's heads. It was not that they were not clear. They were just too intellectual. I listened with obvious interest, and thanked her for the information.

I am thankful the two conversations came close together. I discovered that although people come with different expectations, they all desire to hear a clear message from the Word of God. I decided to do my homework, preach to the best of my ability, and let God do what needed to be done in the lives of the congregation through the preached word. I am learning to put the work I have done into God's hands and let the work of the Spirit of God do with it as the Spirit chooses.

In preaching, we tell and retell the biblical story and its intersection with our lives. We speak not merely of what happened, but of what is happening as God meets us today. For me it is in response to the preached word that I am most vulnerable. Because what I give is a combination of myself and an exposition of a biblical text, I care that the sermon touches people's lives in some way. I am thoroughly blessed when I sense God has taken what I have attempted and made some use of it in a person's life.

Pastors, however, are not mere instructors of the interesting and helpful words of Scripture. People in small churches do not want merely to come to church to hear a lecture. They want to meet the living God. They expect spiritual nourishment and food for the soul. So the Word of God must be known by the parish exegete. But the Word of God must be known for an even more important and pressing reason. It must be known because it brings us face to face with God. We dare not stand before the congregation as a parish pastor unless we have first stood before God as revealed in Scripture. It is here we find the living Lord, the head of the church to which we have been sent.

It is this encounter with the living Lord that people seek. (This is not all they seek through church involvement, but this desire is always there, surfacing sometimes vaguely, sometimes intensely.) There is a correct expectation that the pastor will have a vital relationship with God. It is our duty not only to help people seek the face of the living Lord, but to dispel the rumor that we think we are the only ones who can help this desire to be fulfilled. If we are to exegete correctly, we must enable the people to see not only God, but our frailty and their spirituality as well. We are not the only ones who know the living Lord. But if we do not know God, we will neither enable them to see God nor be able to affirm their own depth of faith. In the small church, we come so that we "may impart to you some spiritual gift to strengthen you, that is, that we may be mutually encouraged by each other's faith, both yours and mine" (Rom. 1:11-12).

■ **III** ■

The parish exegete must know the congregation. As each pastor is unique, so each parish is unique. The intersection of the pastor and the parish will define ministry for a particular time and place. We must learn the histories, the glory days, the low days. We must know something about the former pastor and the place of the church in the community in years past. We must know who these people are and what church and community experiences have created them to be who they are. This is part of the joy of small-church ministry. Stories abound, and the joy of discovering who a congregation is, is part of the joy of ministry.

It is an unearned privilege bestowed on the pastor, because of the tradition of the role, that we enter into the variety and intimacy of the human drama. Previously untold secrets are whispered into our ears. Midnight crisis calls involving only family members include the pastor. Dreams of marriage are often first shared with the pastor, as is the cracking apart of a once-solid love. These secrets are part of the untold story of a congregation.

To know a congregation means to exegete their life, their history, their joys and sorrows, their dreams and failures. It is also to see the richness of their text. In the small church there is the expectation of interest and friendship that the pastor is to have for each member. Our time is spent not on administering large programs or groups of people, but in hearing and responding to the stories in the lives of the members. But the reason to know the stories goes beyond the expectations of the people to the pattern of God's love. God initiates a pattern of interest in lives encountered. As I begin to learn more about a person, often my judgments change and my love increases. We begin to see the depth of faith in unexpected places. Not only is our preaching enriched by these stories (not used as illustrations but to give us greater understanding of the human condition), but our self-understanding increases as well. We mature as we interact with the maturity and immaturity of young and old within the congregation.

One must exegete not only the philosophical, historical, and spiritual components of a small church, but also the statistical. We must know where we live. The small community of Lindsay, California (population eight thousand), in which the small church (membership two hundred, average attendance one hundred) I serve is located, is in the heart of California's Central Valley. The San Joaquin Valley is dotted by small towns, many on the verge of growth, others for which this dream has vanished. These towns are filled with churches, mainline and non-mainline, English speaking and non-English speaking, in our community Spanish speaking. There are twenty-three known churches in Lindsay, and more that meet "unofficially" as small Christian fellowships. In most of these towns there has been a shift in racial makeup, received with varying degrees of acceptance, with which the community of faith is constantly involved.

In many of these small towns there is another mix. It is the mix between the newcomers and the old-timers. A newcomer is one who has recently moved into the area, as recently as last week or the last decade. People who moved into the area twenty-five or more years ago are still thought of as newcomers. They have become significant contributors to the church and the community, but they are still considered new by some old-timers.

Into this mix of old-timer and newcomer the pastor enters. I have wondered at times if pastors are mere pawns of history, who help play out a drama that would go on even without them. After all, those we come to serve have been in this particular church many years. Many have held the hope of faith more intensely than we, and for a span of years that may exceed twice our age. Yet we come, to serve, to listen, to lead. And in the graciousness of God we become part of this complicated mix of people who for various reasons have chosen to associate with the particular local church that has called us.

■ IV ■

The small church is not a small version of a big church. We in the small church cannot expect to run all the same programs and ministries that take place in big churches on grander scales. This was, and continues to be, a struggle for me to accept. I was raised in larger churches, and before moving to Lindsay I had worked in several large congregations. I came to see ministry through certain filters and attempted to use them in structuring ministry in the smaller church. It does not work. In our midweek children's program, for instance, we minister to nearly seventy young people. This number is not far removed from the numbers of children typical of similar programs in larger churches. The difference is that we use a far greater percentage of our people in running this one program, and so do not have the ability to do what we want in other areas of church life. The small church has to choose its ministries more carefully, because more people are needed to run fewer programs. At times we even choose to limit the numbers to whom we minister, in order to lower the rate of volunteer burnout.

The small church in the small community is often an ecumenical gathering of the people of God, from a great diversity of backgrounds theologically, culturally, and genetically. We are a fellowship of those who have responded to the call of God to be partners in ministry. We come from Presbyterian,

Catholic, Methodist, Lutheran, Church of Christ, and Baptist stock, joining together to form a new, unique version of the people of God.

Ministry in a small town surrounded by small and larger towns can be a frightening challenge. It is frightening because our particular town has almost as many people choosing to move out as to move in. Retired people often move to the coast. Young people often move to the closest city, twenty minutes away. The populace from which Presbyterians have traditionally drawn their members is shrinking. The changing face of the community can be frightening.

But such ministry is also challenging. As our little church changes to meet the changing face of our community, we discover the challenge of affirming the gospel's relevance to people of all backgrounds and social standing. We have been encouraged by an unaffiliated Hispanic fellowship that meets regularly in our church facility. Through the work of our presbytery's Hispanic committee, they have recently become an officially recognized Presbyterian fellowship and are beginning to make a move toward becoming a Hispanic Presbyterian congregation. We have a joint Sunday school for our children, and hope to come together in other special activities. This is a sign of progress and hope for us.

As I reflect in general on ministry in a small church, I find I have a love/hate relationship with it. I love the familiarity of the faces I see in the market or at the city festival. I love the acceptance of people within and outside the church. I love the united effort of many churches to minister within the community and the strong presence of Christian people in community affairs. I love the history of a place so affected by those within the church. I love the time given to pastors by the people for learning the ropes. I love the fruit on the porch, and the grafting man in the backyard who arrives unannounced. I love the faithfulness of the older members and the energy of the younger ones. I love dreaming together about how God through us can make a difference in this community.

But there are things I do not love. I do not love the tenacious hold of the past, which remembers "how things were done" and attempts to bring that style into today's world. I do not love the familiarity of the future, which sees the same issues (like whether we should put on a new roof) come up year after year in seasonal succession. I do not love the ambivalence of the present, which resists new possibilities (like having a seminary intern) for fear of lack of finances or potential failure. I do not love the pain of the past (like the tragic death of a child), which has led to a lingering divisiveness. I do not love the problems of the past, which hang ghostlike around the halls of the church. The impact of past problems lingers in a small church, where other problems do not balance them and the longevity of the membership keeps them current.

But I love it that God is, in fact, God, and knows all these issues, where they will take us, what we will do with them, and how we will be better able to be the church in this community because of them. I love it that in the intersection of parish exegete and congregation the Word of God is alive and leading us to a full tomorrow, whether through difficult waters or through joyful encounters. The call to the small church is a uniquely challenging and rewarding call. It is God's call, with great challenges and deep rewards.

■ 12 ■

Retiring into Ministry

John L. Anderson

THE CHURCH STANDS at the crossroads, almost. Precisely at the northeast corner of the crossroads is the Grange Hall, with the church higher on the hill next door. For all practical purposes the Grange Hall serves as the parish hall of the congregation. There potlucks are served, wedding receptions held, and all sorts of celebrations and fairs of the wider community take place. The main road runs north and south. The road going west ends in a mile or two in a farmyard of a pillar family of the congregation. The road east, after crossing the main foothill highway, soon forks into roads skirting the foothills in one direction, and in the other runs along the edge of the canyon overlooking the main river of the region. Between this river and a main tributary that flows in a canyon of the lands of the farm family mentioned above lies a high, relatively flat plateau. The community the church serves extends along that plateau for eight or ten miles. About five miles to the north, along the main foothills road, on the north side of the river, is a small town, the hub of the whole area. All the children of the surrounding communities are bused to the consolidated school in the town.

A hundred yards up the main road is a country store, dispensing the usual wares: gasoline, feed and seed, and some hardware and groceries. Between the store and the church are two homes of church people, one of which is the manse, currently rented out, with the income used to support the budget of the church.

JOHN L. ANDERSON *is professor emeritus of religious studies, Lewis and Clark College, Portland, Oregon. Following his retirement from teaching, he served as pastor of Springwater Presbyterian Church in Estacada, Oregon. He is now retired and living in Portland.*

■ I ■

In location the church should be classed as rural. It lies near the center of the plateau, with adjoining communities higher and lower on the long plateau. The membership of the congregation, however, is hardly rural in the traditional sense of the word. Only one family at the present time extracts its entire living from the land. Much of the area is broken up in small tracts and lots of twenty to forty acres. Much is produced on some of these tracts, but it is supplemental. Many of the inhabitants are commuters. Others are retirees, refugees from the hurly-burly of the urban center, about thirty miles distant. There are still some ranches left scattered about, but most of them have been divided and subdivided. Many fields, small and large, have been converted to the production of Christmas trees.

In size the congregation carries on the rolls between sixty and sixty-five members. On the whole the membership is well educated. At least two members, one of whom is retired, hold Ph.D. degrees. The one M.D. is also retired, but both retirees are very active. Several members hold master's degrees, and still others teaching credentials beyond the bachelor level. Several others have been or are still in college. There are some professionals in the congregation, serving as teachers, counselors, accountants, or forest service personnel. One helpful man of many skills earns his living as a tree-feller. One engineer is retired but somewhat active.

A large portion of the membership is elderly. Several are widows, many of whom are quite active. At the other end of the scale, there is a growing cluster of younger families with small children. At the present time there are few youth of junior and senior high school age.

Beyond the membership there is a wider constituency. Some of these people belong to families who have lived in the community since the early days. The church celebrates its one hundredth anniversary in 1991. Others are more recent migrants who have become more or less attached to some church activity, perhaps an Easter service or a Christmas program. A few stalwarts among the above can always be counted on when

113

the church building or the Grange Hall needs special repairs. On occasion one or two of the more affluent of these friends will contribute money as well as time to special projects. Recently the manse was refurbished by a concerted effort of these members and friends, male and female. A local architect's assistant, a nonmember of a member family, was employed to direct the project.

In addition, there were neighbors who attended other churches of the wider area, usually "conservative" or "evangelical," of which there are many. Many others in the neighborhood could not care less. Indeed they tend to shun any human association. Some of these had fled the city. Others, some of whom live in substantial homes, were active church members, but they now resist any intrusion in their chosen isolation. In traveling the back roads in the vast areas of second-growth timber, one finds a fair number of antisocial types who much prefer their own company. Usually one encounters vocal dogs who vigorously challenge any attempt to intrude on the hideaway.

The social world of a fair segment of the local population can be discerned by observing the universal mode of transportation—a pick-up truck, often four-wheel drive. In the back of the cab hangs a fishing rod or two, a gun or two. The body of the truck usually contains a tool box, perhaps a saddle or an axe, or a shovel—and often a large dog that has learned from experience how to maintain a steady balance as the master careens at high speed along the narrow mountain roads. On weekends, many of these local citizens will be found during the appropriate season hunting or fishing. Another fair number will be found at the local golf course, where on any given Sunday a church member returning home can compare the number of parked cars there with the number in the church parking lot. On more than one occasion, the pastor and his wife have made the daily constitutional along the border of the golf course following the morning service, and the former has been sorely tempted to express himself to the latter by some snide comment relative to the morning attendance.

I had become acquainted with some members of the congregation over several years. One Easter morning, the pulpit being vacant, I was asked to preach. After the service, the man who invited me and who also happened to be a colleague of many years who had moved into the community and become active in the church, suggested that I consider candidating. After some months of reflection, I accepted the invitation. It had been many years since I had spent any time as a pastor, and then only during summer months while in college or seminary. So the new experience was challenging, exciting, and threatening, all at the same time. I was to invest 40 percent of "full time" to this ministry. I never tried to check on the hours I spent during the five years I served.

■ **II** ■

Over some years of pew-sitting and periodic interim preaching, I had developed some convictions about worship and, in particular, the role of the sermon. In addition, my experiences in the classroom and pulpit led me to concentrate on a general expository style, and from the beginning I thought it best to use the Common Lectionary, at least most of the time. Usually I chose to focus on one of the readings for the day, but to vary the diet I would try to weave together a commentary using all of the readings, including the psalm when appropriate. I used the liturgical year to plan series of sermons, particularly for Advent and Lent. To vary the routine, I tried to pick, for a month or six weeks, texts from a single book. I took some pains to deal with the backgrounds of the work. As I look back on it, I wonder sometimes whether perhaps too often I spent more time explicating what the writer intended to say than what the text could say today to all of us. Always the attempt to bring home a timely message out of the passage was most difficult for me. I was often tempted to open up the possibilities of the text in such a way as to allow the hearer to make her and his own application. On the other hand, when I sought to be more explicit with some relevant application, I fear that overfrequently it bore down on a common theme: the sinfulness of humankind, especially corporate sin.

Early in the first weeks, one of the elders approached me and gently suggested that for him my sermons tended to be "rather complicated." He went on to volunteer, if I did not object, to provide a white board behind the pulpit on which I could outline the main points of the sermon. I resisted any temptation to defend my sermonizing. I accepted the idea, and from then on I found the device quite useful. It helped me to be quite explicit in my organization and thus freed me from my notes to allow me to speak more directly to the congregation in a sort of "face-to-face" manner. All that forced me to sharpen my memory. Of course it failed me at times, and sometimes on Sunday afternoons or even the next day, a particularly relevant illustration or telling point would well up and I would realize that I had forgotten the bit. An occasional feeling of futility was not helped by these slips. Indeed, once in awhile I wondered whether my, or anyone's, sermons accomplished much.

While the sermon was the center of my attention and study, it was an integral part of the whole worship service. In my earlier years, I had spent some time in the study of the Reformed worship traditions, and I had come to a rather "high" church conviction about its structure and form. I adopted readily the denomination's proposed "Service for the Lord's Day." An elder had a trial form of the proposal, and when she put it into my hands, I was delighted. To gather to praise and glorify God, to be confronted by God's Word, and to be refreshed and renewed for the next encounter with the world around us seemed to me to be a most direct and simple pattern. I felt it imperative to be careful about the very beginning of the service. I worked hard to bring off just the right tone and touch to the prayer of adoration. For this I could not trust my memory, but in composing just the right words, I feared my efforts came off as too much studied composition. I never did feel easy about it.

The congregation did not use a bulletin and gently resisted my suggestions to do so. I felt hampered in my efforts to involve the people at appropriate places. The elder who had supplied the draft of the "Service for the Lord's Day" came to my rescue. She suggested that I work out a series of worship services, varying the prayers of confession and the sung responses that I wanted to introduce, along with the other items that invited congregational participation. Soon I worked out a half dozen of these. They were printed on good quality paper and then laminated with a thin sheet of plastic film. Each one was in a different color. They turned out to be a helpful substitute for the usual bulletin.

Fortunately the congregation loved to sing, and it wasn't long before we had used more hymns, new and old, than they had ever used before. Many could read music readily. So we did not really miss a choir, although for special seasons we formed one. When that happened, a good share of the congregation was in it. Again fortunately we had a good organist, who appreciated variations on the familiar, provided that the structure did not vary much. The skill of the congregation allowed me to introduce with little difficulty sung responses and canticles. We did encounter some hesitancy in altering the response to "In Jesus Christ we are forgiven." From time immemorial it had been the traditional "Gloria Patri." But the message came fresh and new as we became accustomed to verses of familiar hymns or new texts to express our gratitude. We used the same pattern for our communion services, which averaged about six times a year. We sought to introduce sung responses at the appropriate places in the Great Prayer, but these efforts were less successful. Perhaps we did not do them often enough to be implanted in the memory. Furthermore we received a rather solid resistance to any tampering with the form of the Lord's Prayer. On the other hand, variations on the creedal affirmations following the sermon met no appreciable objection.

As I have previously hinted, the more difficult parts of the worship services for me were the prayers. In a way I was consciously or unconsciously trying to use the prayers as a device to encourage the members to do their own praying. I was fearful of free spontaneity—remembering all too well the repetitions and stereotypes I had listened to in my youth.

The People's Prayer tended to slip into a certain sameness. This I tried to resist. The "joys" and "concerns" were parochial. Nonetheless these often provided me with suggestions and tips for pastoral calling. In my share of the prayer, I tried to extend the boundaries of our concerns. On some occasions I varied the format, using different thematic responses or suggesting various topics to be followed by a period of silence, then concluding with a brief collect.

■ III ■

Many of the church members were also members of the Grange. That association offered much of the support and caring the members provided for one another as well as those beyond the membership. Nonetheless, the church's fellowship chair planned programs for members and friends, usually on mission topics, local or worldwide. One of our active widows served as a volunteer in mission at Sheldon Jackson College in Alaska, and that provided an excellent program, to cite one of them. On the whole, though, attendance was spotty, especially at evening programs. Other forms of fellowship came in the package with which we are all familiar—shared meals. The most notable of these took the form of a progressive dinner in which one family would provide the hors d'oeuvres, another the soup, another salad, and so forth, ending up with the usual coffee and dessert. Almost the entire membership participated. The highest quality of fellowship occurred, however, after every morning service. Usually most of those in attendance lingered long over modest refreshments and lengthy interaction.

■ IV ■

From the outset, pastoral calling claimed a high priority, next to worship. It may have been a dangling flash of memory from seminary homiletics class that nudged me in this direction. As I recall it, I heard the professor say something to the effect that effective preaching was built upon intimate acquaintance with the flock. Thus from the beginning my ministry in the small church centered around two activities: study at home and calling during my weekly visit to the parish. Fortunately

I inherited an able chairperson of the outreach committee. She was a widow in her late fifties or early sixties who knew most of the people, or if she did not know them, was as eager as I to make their acquaintance. Moreover she loved to drive, and what was more, she knew how to get where we needed to go. To cap it all off, she knew when to stay in the car or let me drive by myself to go it alone. Thank heaven she was on hand at the start of the whole process.

It was quite difficult for me at first. I am not one who is at ease with strangers, nor is it easy to make new acquaintances. Yet I knew that it had to be done, so I plunged in to call systematically on all the families of the parish. That did not take too long, and soon priorities fell into place. The ill, the infirm, the houseridden were always sought out at first. At intervals single persons who lived alone received calls.

To initiate conversation, too, was cumbersome to me. The usual trivia was apt to follow the introduction that helped to identify who I was. In time deeper concerns surfaced. Offering prayer or snippets of moralistic admonition were not part of my normal style. Of course I soon came to sense when prayer or silence or a line or two from a psalm was welcomed. For the most part, after becoming aware of the interests, or work, or pressing problems of the parishioner, I felt more confident about what might be helpful. But it wasn't easy.

Hospital calls were usually few and far between. From my own experience, and especially at the insistence of my wife, who was quite adamant on the subject, I determined that ordinarily such calls be on the short side. That became the norm. A sense of presence and a personal concern were communicated. But fresh stages of a disease or of healing produced variance. I tried hard to be sensitive and never tire a patient.

The hardest calls were those associated with terminal illness. Usually it was cancer. Two lingering cases came rather close together and both involved women in late middle age. I soon became aware that the whole families were in need of some comfort and assurance in the face of the unknown and often dreaded the future. In one case I was confronted with a brave front, and it was genuine enough, but it proved fragile in the end. My own need led me to seek help from a knowledgeable colleague in the neighboring parish of the same denomination. She had had recent training and proved most helpful. As it turned out in one case, I had to be absent, and in my stead, she became a frequent and welcome visitor. Through the joint services of our congregations she had already become acquainted with a number in our congregation. The lay leaders had come to have confidence in her, and when I had to be absent for any extended period of time, she was called in and was always welcomed by those she served. Her assistance was invaluable to me.

Another source of help came from members of the lectionary group to which I was invited. Two of those pastors had had training in crisis or drug-related counseling. Their advice and comment were also quite helpful to me. One of them, a Methodist, had been a student of mine in his college days. The members of the group were somewhat younger than I, and they often relied on me for critical comment on the passages for the week.

My calling reached beyond the parish. The congregation had made it a practice, when without a pastor, for elders to call on both members and neighbors of long-standing relationship to the community. I was glad to inherit the task. That was the kind of nurturing a small congregation in that situation should naturally assume. In addition, in a more or less systematic way I called on every one in the area who offered any likelihood of becoming a new member. Of course I met people who welcomed my visit but indicated that they had other commitments. Once in a while I ran across people who seemed quite hostile and abrupt. Here and there such visits sparked an interest and resulted in new memberships—not enough, however, to reach what I regarded as the potential. Others might attend for a while from time to time, but usually these folk just ceased to come. I tried to continue a relationship with them even when they moved from the area. Somehow a fair number of people simply did not care to respond or vary their mode of life.

■ V ■

Before I became the pastor of the church, I had been involved in both ecumenical and interfaith relations. At the urging of a former student who had become a semiretired local pastor in the town, I began to attend the monthly meetings of the local ministerial association. I tried to cooperate in various affairs such as the annual Thanksgiving service or our periodic attempts to rally a few folk into coming together to sing portions of the *Messiah*. Much of the monthly meetings, however, seemed to be filled with low-level concerns such as whatever was going on at city hall or the behavior of some of the high school youth. Little attempt was made to schedule more substantial subjects—counseling problems, biblical studies, book reviews, or liturgical experimentation—all of which I was prepared to invest in. So I soon gave it up as a general waste of time and travel.

With two other congregations, one the local Methodist church and the other a fellow Presbyterian, we cooperated on special events during Advent and Lent. And in the summers, we sponsored a joint summer day-camp for the younger folk. A local mission project seemed to foster a sustained involvement on the part of a few loyal and dedicated laypeople. It started out as an extension of our regular participation in a program to feed needy families in the area. Collection of foodstuffs had already become a regular part of each of our worship services. Other congregations joined in this as well. The new venture was sparked by an invitation on the part of the hunger program of the presbytery. The Church and Society Committee had agreed to fund to a modest amount a few innovative mission projects that seemed to meet new local needs. One of our lay leaders suggested a need for a survey of the growing number of homeless people along with better information concerning the need for fuel and clothing for the coming winter among those living a precarious existence in the area. When the presbytery agreed to fund the survey, the other congregations with which we regularly cooperated were invited to participate. A startling number of people with inadequate or no shelter were found. A wider committee was established when a fourth congregation joined the effort. Soon it was determined that some kind of shelter must be provided, even if temporary. The town leaders were alerted and tendered some assistance. A house was located and procured. Donations of

121

furniture and blankets and clothing followed. More funds were raised. A part-time manager was engaged. But alas, when all was ready and volunteers procured for the first week of the operation, the health officials determined that one bathroom was inadequate for housing male and female clientele at the same time. About this time the manager resigned and the project came to an abrupt halt.

Shortly after this my time of service came to the end. I can report that the termination of the project, after so much effort, resulted in widespread disappointment. On the other hand, all the participants discovered rewards in terms of learning in an ecumenical setting to share the joys and pains of a pioneering mission effort—but no house.

■ VI ■

A capable lay leadership in the congregation had developed over a number of years. A sensitivity to the wider mission of the church had been a high priority for some time. That matter appeared to be the chief concern at budget time. Except for presenting a sermon on the subject, I did not feel the necessity of becoming involved. I did indeed feel strongly about the need for generous giving and eagerly voiced this in the sermon. I did, however, participate more actively in one stewardship campaign, the last one held after I had tendered my resignation. A fair increase in the budget for the coming year loomed as a necessity in order to support the new pastor. Presbytery's Committee on Ministry had helped the pastor-seeking committee to see the possibility of tapping additional resources. This led to a judgment that the congregation could raise its contribution to the pastoral budget to 60 percent. Furthermore, since my remuneration was limited by the regulations of the pension board, and the new pastor's salary had to come up to presbytery's minimum, that portion of the budget called for a sizeable increase. All this led to the decision of the church's governing body that a full-blown, well-planned stewardship campaign was in order. My actual participation was more symbolic than substantial, however. The local leadership seemed to be adequate. Indeed, it was superior. In the first effort of this sort in years, the campaign came close to its goal.

■ VII ■

In terms of a total program for children, leadership for the educational program of the church fell far short. There were plenty of qualified leaders. In fact, the congregation as a whole was rich in leader potential. But a number of conditions collaborated to defeat the possibilities. First and foremost, there was not a large number of children to enable us to offer even a broad grouping on a steady, dependable basis. The children were sporadic in attendance. Many of the leaders had served in previous years, a few for a fair number of years, and they felt they had burned out. A handful of dedicated women, however, agreed to take turns in preparing the lessons and activities for two broad age groups of grade school children. Attendance was irregular, however, and this tended to discourage students and teachers. No one could be persuaded to assume the job of education chair during the last three of my five years of service.

There was plenty of talent available for the adult phase of the program. Since this was in line with my major interests, I was happy to take on a good share of it. My classes were entirely biblical. Most of the time I taught the nine o'clock class on Sunday mornings. The faithful members of that group had good background for fairly advanced material. Occasionally a topic would arouse wider interest and the numbers would increase. When the group wanted a change, qualified lay persons stepped in and offered a course or two, a memorable one being "When bad things happen to good people."

I experimented with classes at other times. Midweek attempts were not well attended as a whole. For a time a faithful few gathered for discussion and prayer using the *Mission Yearbook of Prayer and Study*. We met at different homes for this. Two other projects turned out well. Both were scheduled for later on Sunday afternoons. They ran for an hour and a half. One was a beginning overview of the Bible. The other dealt with major theological themes of first the Old Testament and then the New. Both these courses extended over about two months. Attendance held up well. All this made a long day for me, however.

The congregation responded to educational programs offered by the presbytery. The church provided generous scholarships for attendance for both adults and youth. For myself, I took advantage of the funds provided for continuing education. Courses offered on the lectionary for the special seasons of Lent and Advent I always attended. Most were helpful. One was a miserable failure. I also taught Bible courses for two summers at the annual Presbyterian Conference.

■ VIII ■

The brief experience I had in leading a small congregation was indeed personally rewarding, if not all of the time pleasurable. The pleasures came with meeting wonderful people and sharing their responses. It was a personal enrichment for my wife and me to share the lives, the hopes, the frustrations, and the despair of such people. I had my share of disappointments and defeats. Too often I failed to find the right key to aid in mending marital breaches. On the other hand, one effort at a long and patient nurturing resulted in a reconciliation. Very rewarding.

Frustration attended my efforts at including the children in the worship services. I even took a two-day short course on how it might be done. For a good share of the first year I carefully prepared a time for children. At times it went well. But attendance was sporadic. After several occasions when preparations were unused due to lack of attendance, I threw in the towel.

A large portion of the feeling of unfulfillment for me came from my not living in the community. Try as I might to be on hand for emergencies and crises, I was not always available. This hurt when accidents or deaths occurred. We just were not part of the living community. I felt a certain social distance when one long-slumbering family difference surfaced for a time. Close as that family was to the life of the church, I felt put off at arm's length from searching for the root of the matter. I hung on, spent time and effort. Though it seemed that a certain degree of reconciliation took place, and though the moment of exchanging the peace the next Sunday reverberated with deep undertones, I could feel the resolution was not lasting. In a rural area where neighbors take care of one another, the pastor needs to be on hand to contribute his or her share.

My experience leads me to the conviction that the denominations need to take better care of the small churches. Denominational officers can be a great source of loyalty and solid commitment. Part of the difficulty, of course, is the scandal of unequal remuneration of the clergy. Leaders of small congregations cannot command sufficient resources to give their children education anywhere equal to their own. In my early years following my ordination, I had a rich experience in the Highlands of Scotland. The country parish I came to know had excellent leadership. Two lads of the manse were enabled not only to attend the university but to go on to graduate school. Equalization of salaries in part made this possible. Surely our church in rich America, if it put its mind to it, could find a way of meeting such needs.

13

A Ministry of Change

Julio A. Ramirez

TWO YEARS AGO, Guadalupe Quinonez, then seventeen, began to read the Bible with me, as we became friends in the English program offered by the new Hispanic Protestant ministry in East Oakland.

From the beginning, he looked on me and talked with me as though I were his older brother. He shared many of his pains and his loneliness. He was a recent arrival in the United States and was living with an older brother who constantly humiliated him, criticized him, and prevented him from going to a Protestant church. Guadalupe often missed his mother and told me about how he had hardly known his father, whom he had visited in Islas Marias, the island jail off the coast of Mexico. He later mentioned that when his father was finally released from prison, he did not even bother to go visit his wife and kids.

Guadalupe told me about his dreams. He wanted to be "legally" in this country, because he wanted to study—he wanted to go to college one day. I told him not to be desperate, that some changes would begin to take place if he trusted God and took all his dreams seriously. He did not see much hope sometimes. I did not see many possibilities to help his situation. But I told us both to be patient, something would happen, something would change in our lives.

Now, two years later, Guadalupe and I sit laughing and reminiscing about what has happened here, with joy and deep satisfaction. With the help of this ministry, Guadalupe is now in the last stages of becoming a fully "legalized" (documented) alien, he has a work permit, he has moved from our English

JULIO A. RAMIREZ *is the pastor of the Iglesia Presbiteriana Hispana in Oakland, California.*

as a Second Language program to the nearby community college (as seven other young people from our community have done), and he has learned to play the guitar. And he has learned to take pictures and is our official *fotografo* who documents all our activities. He wants to be a music missionary to other churches.

The ministry here has changed, too, in two years. It began with an English program. We are now a worshiping community, two youth groups (school age and young adults), two choirs (one for church hymns and one for *coritos,* or songs sung and accompanied in a Latin-American style), and a Bible study group. We have with us a job cooperative for Central Americans (MANOS) with a membership of over 170. A Mexican folkloric ballet troupe practices and teaches with us. Much has changed, and we continue to change.

■ I ■

During World War II, East Oakland, always a suburb of cosmopolitan San Francisco, was a community with many Portuguese fishermen. Before then it was an area where mostly Germans did agricultural work and raised cattle. After the war, it became a predominantly African-American area, along with other parts of Oakland. About ten years ago another dramatic change began to take place in the population. There were increasing numbers of people speaking Spanish. The big Catholic church in the heart of East Oakland began to have its first masses in Spanish. About 70 percent of its three thousand communicants are now Hispanic.

The main reasons for the growing Hispanic population in East Oakland apply in many other places in this country: the wars raging through Central and South America, for example, and the failing economies of heavily indebted countries, particularly Mexico. East Oakland is only a bridge away from San Francisco, where there is a large and venerable Hispanic community—one far older than the state of California. Oakland receives the spillover from San Francisco, where many arrive from all over Latin America.

127

The move to Oakland makes sense. Because of racial dis-
crimination, African-American communities historically have
tended to be poorer than Euro-American communities, and
hence in some ways less expensive to live in, and that is what
Hispanics can afford. Unofficial estimates put the general racial
makeup of East Oakland at 40 percent black, 40 percent Hispanic, 10 percent Asian, and 10 percent white. This suggests
a Hispanic population of thirty to forty thousand; my own
estimate is well above that.

Census information cannot be taken very seriously. The common experience of seeing several Hispanic families, including
six to eight men and women, living of necessity in a single
apartment forces you to see census data in the same way: in
any inquiry about who lives in any given housing unit, only
a fraction of the people are reported. In any Hispanic community, there are a great many undocumented people, often
up to 50 percent. There are fears of the INS, the owner of the
apartment, and any number of other potentially threatening
authorities.

Whatever the actual numbers of Hispanic people in East
Oakland, the population is dramatically changing. Thirty years
ago, the Anglo congregation whose building we share for our
new church development had twelve hundred members. Today
it numbers some sixty white members, mostly in their sixties
and seventies. The old chapel is now rented to a black Baptist
congregation. There has been a population shift.

White people have moved to the edges of this colorful community of East Oakland. They have set geographical limits
around the edges that sometimes become offensive because
the difference between one side and the other is so dramatic.
These limits include the canal that divides Oakland from Alameda, and the freeway I-580, which as a limit has become
less obvious and begun to erode, as has the city limit between
Oakland and San Leandro. As soon as you cross the short
bridges to Alameda, you see beautiful homes, with well-cared-
for lawns and green areas, clean streets, more police surveil-
lance—if you are from Oakland, you notice the police in two
ways: you see more police, and police see you more. I have a
recent memory of this. One day I got a fine that to me seemed

clearly to mean "You are not welcome on this side of the canal" more than "You committed a traffic violation." One month later, the judge agreed with me.

On the Oakland side, old white folk still talk with some resentment about the colorful newcomers taking over their East Oakland town and churches. I continue to hear stories about the glorious days when this area was pretty, clean, prosperous, less ethnic.

■ **II** ■

In comparison with the Hispanic district in San Francisco, East Oakland is the poorer. It does not have many old established Hispanic families in business and industry. Another characteristic that is quite different from other Hispanic communities I know of, such as San Diego, Los Angeles, and San Francisco, is that here Hispanics and African-Americans live side by side with each other. In any given block, you will find that one home is black and one Hispanic. There are some clusters of Hispanic or black homes or an apartment building that has mostly one or the other, but such concentration exists at this time only on a very small scale.

Most of the Hispanics are recent arrivals. Many are from Central America, mostly Salvadorans and Guatemalans. The largest nationality represented continues to be Mexican, but not in such large percentages as you find in Los Angeles, and maybe not so few as in San Francisco, where Mexicans are no longer the majority.

As a result of the war, repression, and the unemployment rate of over 50 percent in El Salvador, there are a million Salvadorans in this country now. Oakland has experienced the effects of this massive influx since about 1980. By new arrivals, I mean people who have arrived in the last five years. This includes people who do not qualify for the amnesty provision of the Immigration Reform and Control Act (IRCA), whose purpose was to grant "legal" residence to immigrants living in this country before 1982, or to field-workers who can prove

129

they worked for at least ninety days between May 1985 and May 1986, or sometime during the preceding three years. For the millions of Latin Americans who have arrived in our cities in the last five years, there is little hope. They will continue to live here, because they cannot and will not go back, because they fear they will be killed, or because they have nothing to go back to. Millions of undocumented Hispanics have to live in this country with a law that makes them an underground labor force vulnerable to the caprices of unfair employers and exploiters of undocumented hands.

The IRCA had a second purpose: to stop or control the flow of undocumented people across the borders. For this purpose as well as the first, it has failed miserably. According to the Center for Border Studies of Northern Mexico and the University of California in San Diego's Center for United States–Mexican Studies, the "illegal" crossings have not decreased but increased since the passing of the new immigration law.

The positive result of IRCA is that about four million people will receive a new "legal" (documented) status during the next two years. Many people in this community have benefited and now experience life for the first time without many of the great fears they once faced. As a whole, however, the community continues to suffer. Many relatives and friends did not qualify and see their future in limbo, a life of exploitation and misery.

■ III ■

For these and other reasons, East Oakland stood out as the right location for a Presbyterian Hispanic new church development. In September 1986 I arrived in Oakland to start a church.

Not long before, I had conducted a feasibility study for the United Methodist church in this area. I concluded that the only choices Hispanics had here for church affiliation were a host of small and separate Pentecostal churches, most in vacant store fronts, and the several big Catholic churches, which offered much but could hardly offer community to all their members. Many remained outside any church, yet were hungry for spiritual nourishment. Since the traditional middle class congregations were engaged in practically no ministry among Hispanics in East Oakland, this seemed to offer a potential third choice. I recommended that a socially oriented ministry would be an appropriate way to start a community of faith in this area that was so socioeconomically deprived.

The Methodist church asked me to start the ministry out of a Presbyterian church. Right away I told them this was never going to work: rarely has one lone pastor been able to do the work required in this kind of poor Hispanic community. They agreed and followed my recommendation to join forces with the Presbyterian church, which was also looking to support a Hispanic ministry in this area. At first both denominations agreed that if the ministry were to have any kind of success it would take the work of two pastors: one for outreach in the community and one for the "religious" aspects of ministry, together working as a team. As so often happens, however, the agreement unfortunately did not hold, and the project became Presbyterian alone before a year was out. The people of the community scarcely noticed these negotiations. As far as they were concerned, my presence represented a single multifaceted ministry from its inception.

Thus I arrived and was given the keys to an empty office on the second floor of High Street Church, together with the charge to start a Hispanic congregation.

Trying to figure out my strategy, or my first moves, or maybe to gather up some courage, I spent the first month ordering Bibles and hymnbooks, designing my stationery and personal calling card, getting the telephone connected, and arranging the books on the shelves. Unavoidably, however, I finally had to get started with the actual ministry with and to people.

How to start? If this was to be an organized church, no matter how small, I would have to have people to talk to, a small governing body or steering committee to consult with, to get information from, to plan the first steps with, or to amuse and excite with my enthusiasm and my ideas and methods of ministry. So my friend Luz Estela and I decided to distribute letters to the first eighty homes around the church that had Hispanic names on the mailboxes. Many were hand delivered, so we had a chance to invite personally some of the neighbors, at least those who did not reject us immediately for being Protestant. In these letters we introduced the new Hispanic ministry arriving in the community, invited everybody to share ideas about what we could do together empowered by the Holy Spirit and armed with the love, justice, and peace of God in our hearts. We invited people to come to a dinner and Bible study on the next Wednesday evening.

The appointed time arrived, filled with expectation and excitement—on our part. The food was delicious, a dazzling Colombian *arroz con pollo* (spicy chicken with rice). But nobody from the community showed up.

This was my worst fear—not only that nobody would show up, but that I would be forced to entertain the possibility that my ideas and approaches were not adequate. Have I adopted an Anglo mentality that is unbefitting the Hispanic community? Have my thinking and strategizing been too long related to books, high theology, and artificial schooling? Why did I not connect?

I began to review what could have gone wrong. I thought that probably Paulo Freire or Gustavo Gutiérrez would have told me, "Julio, don't offer to people what you think they need. Let them tell you what they actually need, and then try to give it to them." So immediately I reviewed the feasibility study to remember what kinds of things people wanted. I went to the streets and asked people in the Mexican market and the taco stands what they thought would be helpful to them that the church could do. Some said that what I could do for them is leave them alone, because they were Catholics. Some were courteous about it and some very rude. That was fine, said I.

But some people told me they were afraid about the repercussions of Voter Proposition 63, the infamous "English-only" ballot measure that had recently been passed. I got a lot of requests for English classes, among other things. Many of these people, usually the more outspoken of those I talked with, were women, women with a lot of children around them. So I spent the next days posting about a hundred flyers all over the area announcing an evening English class with free child care. One week later, by the third evening of instruction, I was teaching my own almost-okay English to about forty-five adults, many of them women who for the first time could get away from the chores of the house and childrearing. Meanwhile my missionary friend was taking care of about thirty very happy and loving children.

More people came in the following weeks. We split into two levels of teaching with the help of a Methodist friend. We also had a long social coffee break with Mexican pastry in between the two hours of instruction, where people began to develop good friendship and camaraderie. With great joy we saw before our eyes a community of some sort being born, developing.

It did not take long before we held our first fiesta. People called this the "Community of the English Class." People wanted to be together for more than the classes. We had picnics and trips to the beach, and fiestas to celebrate just about anything. It interested me that nobody ever brought to any of these outings and fiestas the customary alcoholic beverages. People had much respect for the three Christian leaders of this community and gave us little presents on the least occasion possible.

From the beginning people used to approach me to say, "Julio, I know that there is more than English being taught here. I feel you are doing something else, and whatever it is I want to help you with it." To each such person I would give a Bible—good thing I had ordered them—and ask them to read it.

I clarified to the people early on that I was a pastor sent to the area to start a community of faith, but that in order to know people I had to earn my acceptance and the people's trust by helping the community. I made it a point to clarify that they were not going to be getting any unrequested religious instruction in the English classes. "You came for English and English we are going to give you." But we cannot help giving it to you, I would add, as Christians. "I want to be a pastor in this community, and you can come to me for any other kind of help you may need. No matter what it is, come to me."

Sure enough, people began to ask me for translations, information about immigration, legal and medical referrals, and of course some for advice and help on very personal, spiritual matters. People began to emerge who did not think that I should do all the organizing by myself. They formed a support committee. They even named the community. Of all the suggested names, they chose Bartolome de las Casas, the sixteenth-century bishop of Chiapas and Guatemala who defended the cause and lives of the Indians oppressed by the Spanish conquistadors.

Every evening that we gathered, we passed on announcements about jobs, the latest information about the new immigration law, and other needed information. At one point I announced that because some of the people had talked to me about their Christianity and their church, and had shown interest in reading the Bible with me, we would now have a Bible study group that would meet for a light meal and study on Wednesday evenings. I made sure people understood that the invitation went out as well to evangelicals, Catholics, and people of other faiths, and of course to atheists.

Quite as expected, all these groups were represented at the first meeting. There were about fifteen people in all. I could not help thinking of that first Bible study I had announced months earlier that nobody came to.

The meetings continued regularly. We had up to twenty-five adults, plus their children, in our Bible study fellowship dinner. We sang, we prayed, we ate, we talked and studied the Bible in a dynamic way. Liberation theology was central in our studies, because it had been central to me in seminary and since then. This was my first chance, however, to show off my knowledge of theology, Christology, anthropology, and so on. People were excited about this liberation emphasis they had not really heard before: God as liberator, Jesus as a spirituality that moved us to do community work and advocate just causes. They discovered a God that told us we should not be afraid of the gringos even if they were dressed in green (referring to the dreaded Immigration and Naturalization Service).

People felt that God was definitely there in everything we were doing. Moreover, this was a God that chose to be evident through tireless energy to teach English, share information and help with immigration problems, be a friend who could teach guitar or photography, help in getting a restriction order, do a translation, and explain socioeconomic realities that opened eyes and made people move from feeling poor and worthless to feeling impoverished by unjust social structures and the people who benefited from them, and to having reasons to hope for a way out. This was a God that was definitely there, but that chose not to be spoken of much, but mostly shown, in an attempt to be known for what God does.

This is the God that attracted the unchurched, the Mormons, the atheists, and the conservative evangelicals to our Bible studies. This is the God that attracted to our studies the people who are perhaps the most difficult of all to relate to, the "Virgin and saint worshiper" Catholics who in the Hispanic community usually continue to see Protestants as the lepers in town.

The community grew in many ways over the first months. In March the planning committee of our Comunidad Bartolome de las Casas decided, while planning for a trip to Santa Cruz on the Pacific coast, that it was time to start the church for "the Christians" in the Comunidad. The *directiva* included several members of the parish of the largest Catholic church in the area (one of them the secretary of that church), two active members of the Seventh-Day Adventist church, a member of a Pentecostal church, my Presbyterian friend, and several people who were unchurched and nonbelievers. All these supported the idea of holding a first worship service, to which we would invite the whole community of the English class to inaugurate the latest "program" of the community—a Sunday religious service.

Earlier the planning committee had been involved in putting on other events and programs for the community. We held a seminar on violence at home. A psychologist came and for several hours talked to about fifteen women who shared their experiences and cried. Some women had been abused by their husbands when they began to come to English classes. There were violent reactions and family problems related to jealousy and insecurity on the part of the men. As a result of this seminar, a women's group was formed. They met a few times, to plan further events. It disbanded before long, however, in part because of pressure from the men, in part because women had too much work to do, English classes to attend, and all the rest.

The latest program, however, the first worship service, was in any case a success. About ninety people attended this first service. Almost half of them were from our Comunidad. The rest were friends and supporters from other churches.

Worship services have continued uninterrupted ever since. However, in the ensuing Sundays, we had five to eight people in our worship services. The English classes continued to be crowded. The Bible study was well attended. But few of these people showed an interest in committing themselves to the church by becoming a part of the Sunday worship group.

As the more religious aspects of the Comunidad developed and worship played an increasingly important role, the former *directiva* disbanded. They felt they could not remain central in this new church development. Some realized that, if the religious and church aspects had finally become essential, they had their own churches to help. Others simply felt that the religious aspect was not their cup of tea. Some remained and formed the guitar choir for the Sunday service, often outnumbering the people sitting in the pews.

Another development was the youth group. Kids from mostly Catholic families have met regularly every week. They do not necessarily attend our worship on Sundays, since they go to the Catholic church with their parents, who are my friends from the English classes. They have taken a great step by trusting their children to me, but some of them still see an ocean between the Catholic church and Protestant church. This is an ocean created not only by the Catholic church ecclesiastically, but also by the mainline Protestant church racially, ideologically, culturally, and economically.

I know this because I have seen both sides of the ocean. I was born and raised in Latin America. I have been a Catholic, albeit nominally for the most part. I have lived in this country on and off for thirteen years, and so I know what it is like to act and feel like you are not one of the poor, and all that comes with that mentality. I have known about real misery in my childhood and youth. Once again it is a personal experience, as I am part of a people who collectively are living in misery of the ugliest kind.

Now I say I am a Protestant. A believer in and defender of the Reformed tradition, of Calvinism. A product of sorts of the Protestant work ethic and the educational system of this society. But how have I changed? Do we Hispanics change in this society? Or what is it in us that really changes? How do we Hispanics live in the middle of such an immense ocean? Always looking both ways, at the shore of what we are, and at the shore of what we are expected to be. Do we change what is around us, which at times we feel has our essence, or do we give in and become one of the land? What do we keep, and what do we give up? Is it all or nothing, a matter of choosing sides? Just as everything and everyone changes, we must change too. At times it seems that even God changes— God's church certainly does. For the last couple of decades, the poor and the sojourner have become important in the eyes of God's people. Is God changing perspective?

In Oakland many things have changed. The lives of people who were unchurched are now lives with religion at their core. The lives of people who were bound to remain nominally Catholic and Latin-American in their culture and traditions now have discovered a lively Reformed tradition. Now the traditional Protestant church in this area has been changed by a Hispanic–American culture and spirit.

In Latin America we say that "What changed yesterday, will have to change tomorrow." Everything changes. I have changed in spite of all my efforts no to. But two things in this world never change, no matter how good or how bad life becomes—my love for my people, and the memory of our long history of suffering and pain.

■ 14 ■

Pastoral Care Comes to Eagle Creek

Rebecca Hazen

THE AREA I LIVE in seems like the most beautiful in the world. Forty-five minutes from Timberline Lodge on Mount Hood in the Cascade Range, the whole parish is within view of the snow-capped mountain, one mile from a white water river, two and a half hours from the Pacific Ocean, forty minutes from downtown Portland. I am grateful for the privilege of living in the country, because I do not do well surrounded by concrete, asphalt, and traffic.

■ I ■

Before I entered seminary at age thirty-eight, my church experience was in medium-sized churches, with many committees, ongoing programs, janitors, and secretaries. The church I have served for the seven years since seminary has none of that. In our congregation, we act as a committee of the whole, we do only one project at a time, there is no secretary, and each church family takes a turn at being janitor for a month. I type the bulletin for Sundays and drive eleven miles round-trip to run it off on the copy machine at a Methodist church. At our tiny church, however, we do have something larger churches sometimes lack: a high level of personal interest in, and caring about, each other and for any strangers that happen through our doors. There is no way a newcomer can escape

REBECCA HAZEN *is pastor of Eagle Creek Presbyterian Church in Eagle Creek, Oregon.*

out the door after worship without being greeted by at least half a dozen people.

When I first came to this church of thirty-eight souls, I became exasperated by the congregation's inability to pretend it was a medium-sized church. I discovered we could find people willing to work on a special project, but not on an ongoing committee. Here there is little pressure to join and conform. People feel free to do just what they are cut out to do, and are unwilling to expend "organizational energy," which is what you do when you have lots of committees that meet regularly whether they are working on some special project or not. It works best for our congregation and leadership to act as a committee of the whole because everyone wants to know what everyone else in the congregation is thinking before going ahead with a project. As a result, we are unable to move fast on anything, but when we do complete a project, it is because everyone has a stake in the outcome. The pastor's role appears to be as facilitator of the conversations that need to go on among interested parties in order to make the decision. Our style is to talk things over enough until everyone has heard from everyone else, and then we arrive at consensus. We must be careful not to vote too early.

In a small church, the entire congregation can care. One of our members was dying over a period of several months. As I paid pastoral visits on other members of the congregation, they would frequently ask, "What can I do to help?" I could never get many folks to come to an adult education class on how to do lay care-giving, but I became instant educator during such pastoral calls, giving specific suggestions as to what could be done, how someone could support the family, and so forth. This congregation appears to learn more by doing than by education. They prefer not to take the time and effort to attend Bible study class, but they are open to any biblical insight or interpretation I might contribute regarding their particular crisis at the moment.

Three months after accepting the call to serve at Eagle Creek, I called an emergency elders' meeting after worship one Sunday and, without disguising how upset I was, informed them that my marriage was in trouble and they might have a divorced rather than a married pastor. The installation was coming up in a month. It took the elders a mere twenty seconds to respond, "We want you anyway, no matter what." They were confident that the rest of the congregation would feel the same way. That answer for me was an overwhelming experience of the unconditional love of God. Our congregation cares for each person in the same way.

We do ministry together by facilitating people helping people. A retired pastor in the church coordinates the monthly service of a team of volunteers at the senior center. I also help whenever I can and use the time to listen to the elderly of our community and to offer the mealtime prayer. One of our members delivers meals-on-wheels. I consult with the senior outreach worker about connecting the needs of shut-ins with people who can drive wherever or fix whatever. We announce community needs in our "minute for mission" on Sunday mornings. Thus our congregation is seen to care for the community we live in.

Together with a nearby church, we wrote a grant request for money to start a homeless shelter and publish occasional ads in the local paper listing ways readers could help people in need. The manager of the family resource center reports that these periodic alerts are effective.

The congregation went all out to support the three-church youth group when the teens put on a dinner to raise money for the hunger program. Each teen prepared food commonly eaten in a particular country. Then they served it in style to members of the congregation, who made "donations" to the hunger fund as though they were eating at a restaurant. The adults supported the youth in this project by turning out in force, sitting on cushions for Asian and African fare, and acting the part of elegant diners for European fare.

The women of the church work together to raise money, some supplementing the church budget, and some being given to local organizations such as hospice, the community resource center, or the senior center. I participate right along with them when we tie quilts. The monthly meetings provide me an opportunity to listen for situations that might require pastoral care.

Ministry means to be alongside my people whenever they are doing something that is important to them, whether it is with the retired nurse feeding her stroke-disabled husband in the nursing home, or picking berries with the teacher-turned-farmer, or taking a shut-in senior to a movie we can discuss afterwards. I have come to see good pastoral care as becoming an integral part of the people's lives and sharing my faith and how I deal with difficulty to such an extent that they are encouraged to do likewise.

In the seven years I have been with these folks, we have suffered no major conflicts. Perhaps three people came into the church, stayed awhile, did not get their own way, and left feeling injured. The congregation is philosophical about these events, and still loves the persons and is concerned about them, even though they are now absent. The congregation seems to understand that the upsetting issue belonged to the angry person and not to them. They tried to bend to the will of the one person, but soon found their own limits and were willing to speak out about them.

■ II ■

There is an assortment of interests within this body of Christ. Some are interested in the upkeep of the building and keeping things looking nice, others in the Sunday school. Some worry about keeping supplies on hand, or the temperature of the sanctuary on Sunday morning. It took me awhile to understand that not everyone worried about everything. I was expected to worry about everything because I was the pastor. It took me several years to learn not to jump in to rescue every situation, but to see a need, talk to the person with an interest in that need, explain clearly what needed to be done, and thus enable such persons to see themselves using their interests in the service of the church.

One of the joys of serving this church has been the congregation's patience with me as I have learned how to pastor. I think they are so glad to have a regular pastor, living in the manse, after a period of near-death for the congregation, that they were willing to put up with beginner's sermons that had too many points, and with hymns that often were unfamiliar. My way to obtain feedback is to ask for suggestions at elders' meetings. Each member is reminded to listen for needs in the congregation that I might not ordinarily be aware of.

I have grown personally during this time of service. I have read Jungian psychology and spirituality, served as hospice chaplain, and as clergy consultant in a chemical dependency treatment center. Because I support two children besides myself and the church can only afford a half-time salary, "tentmaking" is essential. While at seminary, I watched a hospice chaplain in action with a terminally ill patient. My own father died of Hodgkin's disease when I was eighteen, when the hospice concept in this country was still in its infancy and no one talked of impending death. I saw how effective a hospice chaplain could be in enabling families to face the reality of death together, and felt called to serve in a similar way. Ample opportunity was provided at the beginning of my time in Eagle Creek. A nearby community-based hospice invited me to become their volunteer chaplain. After a couple of years, I left that volunteer position to serve with pay at the home health agency of a health maintenance organization. In time I was encouraged to train as a consultant at a treatment center for alcoholics. In the process I became familiar with the twelve steps of Alcoholics Anonymous. For a while I was working three jobs, and that was too much. For now, I have given up the hospicing. I spend twenty hours a week away from church working in a treatment center twenty-seven miles away. I love the work because I regard it as spiritual direction, and because it keeps me involved in my own twelve-step program for my compulsive overeating. I have come to resent the long commute. But if I am to have my cake of living in a rural setting and eat at all, commuting to an urban area in order to supplement the meager salary appears to be the price I must pay for this privilege of living in the rural setting I love so much.

Eagle Creek cooperates in activities with two other churches, another Presbyterian church ten miles away and a Methodist church five miles away, where the copy machine is located (we share expenses). There is a weekly field trip for kids during the summer, with a van borrowed from a nearby conference center owned by the Methodists. The three-church youth group has five core members, a dozen possible. It meets every other week during the school year. We mail our monthly news-letters together, because two hundred copies are needed for a permit, and we each have fifty to seventy addresses. The three pastors meet weekly for lectionary study. We meet annually on Maundy Thursday for a potluck supper and communion. Last year we did a cooperative "passion play" for this worship service.

The church office is in a corner of my bedroom at the manse, because the place where the office is supposed to be in the church is like a closet. As a result, home life and church life tend to become intertwined. This has been valuable for me as a single parent, because I could study and do office work at home and be present for the children, and do meetings and visits during the day while they were at school. Now that the children are in their late teens, and the church has since obtained a trailer for Sunday school space, I am considering establishing an office in the supply room of the trailer. The lack of secretarial help has frustrated me, since organization, filing, and order-liness are not my strengths. My gifts lie in the areas of pastoral care, counseling, and preaching, rather than administration. But I have come to see administration as a way of leading: pastors are the volunteer coordinator, the shepherd with the staff who guides, or the sheep dog who nips at the heels of the flock. One of my current challenges is to learn to think like a church secretary in order to stay on top of things.

■ III ■

Being a woman in ministry at a small church does not seem to present particular difficulties. The rough edges I have are more related to my personality and style than to my gender. Sometimes folks come to church because I am a woman, per-haps to experience some affirmation of themselves as women. As far as I can tell, my gender has not interfered with how I operate or how I am accepted in the community. In the local ministerial association, although the Assembly of God preacher never spoke out against the ordination of women, he had observed me for the few years he was there. When it came time for him to leave for another placement, his parting remark to me was, "Well, Rebecca, I never did believe in the ordination of women, but you're all right."

The rest of the brethren (literally) appeared to agree. I have come to be known in town as the one who gives specific rather than generic funeral services, and as one who will not marry couples without premarital counseling. I have turned down a few couples for marriage after counseling with them. One such bride-to-be was the granddaughter of one of our lay leaders. I had to confront her about her dominating style. The couple found someone else to marry them, and our member is still speaking to me. Some folks seem to think that the quaint little church in the country is a nice place to get married, but I make lots of referrals to the clerk of court, because I have no interest in running a wedding chapel.

I have chosen to stay here a long time for three reasons: the people, my children, and the setting. I love the people of the congregation and see myself in the role of community builder. I have no need for the status associated with a larger church. I enjoy the advantage of being sole pastor, with command of my time and direct accountability to both the elders and congregation. I do not have to worry about conflict with another staff member. My children have benefited from a stable home after the uproar of divorce. I cherish the scenery, green grass, trees, and running water. I feel connected to the earth here, and with people who are connected to the earth, whether as home gardeners or farmers. Many members of the church have been here forty years, yet they have allowed me to become part of their community and provided me with a sense of extended family. Previously I lived in suburbia, where families moved in and out of the neighborhood frequently and seemed (to me) to be more interested in maintaining an image than in being "just folks." In this rural setting I find an absence of pretentiousness, acceptance of what is, and interdependence, values that are congruent with my own.

To have one pastor for this long period has raised the congregation's self-esteem. Instead of Sunday preachers or seminary interns who left on an annual basis, now there is a pastoral presence available twenty-four hours a day, living next to the church. I have been called in the middle of the night only two times in seven years, and for valid reasons. Whenever people run across a problem that stumps them, they can rely on what is becoming a tradition of consistent pastoral care.

With my ministry, the church has been closely linked to the presbytery and denomination. We receive from them thirty-six hundred dollars of a twenty-thousand-dollar budget. I frequently speak in church about the work of the wider denomination. I participate on committees of presbytery and use denominational materials as much as possible. The congregation was proud that I recently attended the denomination's national assembly as a delegate from our presbytery.

In the course of this ministry, it has become obvious that the spiritual health of the congregation is directly related to my own spiritual health. As I grow in my own faith and speak of it in practical ways, the congregation seems to do likewise. I have come to see my primary role as one of theologian-in-residence, and so I am trusted, even though I am a generation younger than many of the members. When I preach, I open up Scripture and point out options and consequences without being directive. The longer I am here, the deeper it seems become the levels of trust and sharing. It seems that as pastor and parish we could now weather a substantial crisis, due to the quality of our relationship. I believe that in a small church this type of bonding might involve a higher proportion of the congregation than in a large one.

During the past several years I have come to view myself as a spiritual director. My goal is to facilitate people's relationship with God, whether through preaching, teaching, pastoral care, administration, or the example of my everyday life. Integrity is demanded in such a role, and I find I must be in continual internal conversation regarding my behavior, use of time, and attitudes toward people.

During the course of this pastorate I have metamorphosed from a new graduate out to prove herself competent (a typical woman-in-ministry issue), who attempted to please everyone, who was often exhausted and discouraged because she couldn't please everyone all the time, to an able pastor confident of my clarity in teaching and preaching, using my gift of enthusiasm, and seeing my commitment to the church as the body of Christ in the service of this small rural community.

■ 15 ■

Big Bridge
in a Small Place

Philip A. Nesset

THERE ARE TWO common misconceptions in Native American communities. First, many Indians think Christianity is the white man's religion. Second, whites tend to agree with them.

These misunderstandings make room for a lot of trouble today, as they have in the past. But they also present a great opportunity for the church to see itself and its future. A church that sees itself as a support for or mirror of the dominant culture does not have a future. The image of America, wonderful and powerful though it is, is not a worthy substitute for the image of Christ.

For us as Christians, the creativity of the Spirit in other peoples and cultures is a fascinating, complex, engaging process. It is a vital aspect of our vision of the future. It is the work of the Spirit that makes the ministry of our congregation in the Hoopa Valley a delightful challenge.

■ I ■

We Christians have modestly assumed that we have inherited the mantle as the new chosen people. We have reasoned that if it is good to be chosen, then others will benefit from our example. We have received a gift, and we wish to share it and pass it on. To be like us is good. To be us is better yet.

PHILIP A. NESSET *is pastor of the Church of the Mountains in Hoopa, California.*

The good news is perceived through the gift of faith, true enough. But it surely must be of some help to the Spirit if we are thoughtful about what we are saying and what the implications may be. Filled with joy and zeal by the gospel, we are moved to spread the good news. We may be too excited to realize that others have a gift to share with us as well. There may be two or more gifts to be shared. One need not negate the other. In fact, some gifts seem to be enhanced when reflected upon by another.

In times past we have gone to extraordinary lengths to make Indians just like us and, equally important, less like themselves. (Both "Native American" and "Indian" are names given by the colonists. Indians increasingly refer to themselves by their tribal names, much as persons might say they are Polish, Japanese, Palestinian, and so forth.) Few people today realize that during the late 1800s the U.S. government and the major churches of the day divided up the reservations, giving each church not only the right to have missions on the reservations, but to name the superintendents of reservations as well. The violation of the separation of church and state today is mild compared with those days.

Many of the people sent to the reservations by the church were dedicated people. Some were dumped there because no one knew what else to do with them. All shared the conviction that the solution to the Indians' problems lay in helping Indians melt in the melting pot. Native American religion was seen as something akin to devil worship. By the grace of God, Indians have not melted away, and there is a revival in Native American spirituality and Indian pride.

This revival of Indian-ness is hard for people to see. When high school students come to our reservation, the largest in California, they are amazed at how many young people are driving flashy cars. Everyone notices the satellite dishes in yards. Many Indians marry whites. Indians wear the same clothes as the average non-Indian American worker, except for a hat or piece of jewelry that is distinctively Native American. In our cities Indians are often mistaken for Mexicans or Filipinos.

This can have some humor in it. The Indians I know have a good sense of humor. From time to time I will meet one of my members on the street and ask him in a loud voice if there are any "real Indians" around here. Lee is half Irish and half Hupa, but was born and raised in Hoopa and speaks the language. He and his brother attended the BIA (Bureau of Indian Affairs) boarding school that required the children to march across the street in white shirts and dresses to attend chapel at our church. Many resent whites' for that part of our history; others see there is after all a treasure in the very earthen vessel and are presently members of the church.

Recognition has gotten so difficult that one night two elders of the congregation, both members of the Hupa tribe, half seriously considered having the church put up a Great Plains Indian tepee in our backyard. That way outsiders would go home knowing they had *really* been in Indian country.

This may seem silly or irrelevant, but it's not. Several years ago a wealthy congregation elsewhere in the state sent one person to visit us. He returned home with the report that there weren't any Indians here, so why were they sending us money? We were cut off immediately. Perhaps we should have had a tepee.

It is difficult for people to *see* Indians. It is harder still to understand what has happened with them, what is happening, and what the issues are for the future. We too easily leap to the easy conclusion that, all things considered, they must be pretty much like us. If *we* are able to make it, then why can't they?

Massive efforts have been made in the past and continue to this day to make the reservations small economic development zones to provide jobs for people. Billions of dollars have been poured into reservations. Much controversy has arisen over what good this has done, whether funds have been administered, and so forth. But there is, I believe, a growing awareness that even if all these plans and projects had worked, the culture would still be in trouble. In fact it is a culture in crisis.

The irony is that if all the plans and schemes and the like had been successful, the Native American populations and heritages probably would have been lost entirely. As it is, after just one hundred and some odd years of contact with the whites in northern California, many dances, songs, prayers, and ceremonies are having to be reconstructed from written and in some instances recorded sources.

The astounding incidence of alcoholism and other drug abuse, suicides, accidents, and domestic violence has many causes and many consequences. Nevertheless all these problems are worsened by a spiritual vacuum. When individuals and societies lose the Why of life, they lose self-esteem. It has become painfully clear to a growing number of Indians that their spirituality, faith, religion, and ceremonies are essential to their survival. In this respect they seem to be several steps ahead of the rest of society.

Simply injecting know-how and values into reservations and urban Indians isn't really possible or desirable. There have to be ways for both sides to exist and for good bridges to be created and sustained. This is the reason that nation and churches need to maintain the reservation homes at the same time that they reach out to help and support urbanized Indian communities.

Of course supporting both social contexts of the modern Indian's life, reservation and city, takes money and patience, but it is good policy. It is not an easy task. There are economic and political conflicts of interest between resident and non-resident members of many tribes. "That is my home. My heart is still there!" "Yes, but you left, so why don't you leave us alone?" Young people are encouraged to get a good education so that they can help their people, but when they return they find they also are not without honor except in their own hometown. Of course these problems are not limited to Indians.

Through all of this we need to bear in mind that Native Americans see the world in significantly different ways from the rest of us. Since I am not one of them, I would not presume to attempt to explain what is perhaps unexplainable anyway. What I can say is that to wrestle with a worldview that is so different from my own is more than good, it is necessary.

For example, recently a group that included Native Americans and Lutheran clergy, including a bishop, spent more than an hour discussing the qualities of time, whether time is linear or cyclical. If you had the same Old Testament classes in seminary I had, you most likely received the impression that Israel invented the whole concept of history, and that the inferior societies were stuck with cyclical calendars that went around and around and went nowhere.

Now to find within our own country a people who have a more cyclical view of time tied to their love and understanding of their land is a surprise, a mental jolt, a reality-altering perception or insight. This is just one aspect of this ministry that makes it an exciting pastorate.

■ II ■

I have been at the Church of the Mountains for nearly three years. I was raised in Illinois, schooled in Minnesota, am a Lutheran serving a Presbyterian mission congregation, have been ordained twenty years. I have served a six-hundred-member parish, founded a social service agency that died, and dealt in real estate and a few other secular areas. I have been divorced and remarried. I have three girls and a stepdaughter and stepson. My wife works five-eighths time for a university while I am paid to work two-thirds time. There are times when I am able to hold it down to that.

How does a Midwestern Norwegian Lutheran perform his ministry in an ethnic small church mission? I have some assumptions. They are not listed necessarily in order of importance, they tend to blur into one another at times, and some or all may in fact be false. Yet I must have *some* sort of frame of reference.

The first assumption is that those who have gone before me were fairly bright, gifted, dedicated people. This might be called the "humility clause." If things are done in a certain way, if there are problems, if some things don't make sense, the chances are very good that there are reasons for it. Changes will not be made overnight most likely, nor should they be.

Of course this also means that if a problem persists during my tenure I am in good company. Giving full faith and credit to those who have labored before you and to some who now labor with you is only good sense as well as good manners.

I concede that no matter what I say or do, I will never really be a Hupa Indian. The best I can hope for is "honorary" identity, if that. There will always be large areas of life that I will see differently, not understand, be insensitive to. This is perhaps "Humility, Part 2: Self-Taught."

Every congregation has people who will tell you, "We have always done things this way." They are right of course. But when both "things" and "this way" are to at least some degree different from what I know or understand, there are a lot of ways to mess things up.

I understand that while this is my first effort at this sort of ministry, I am not their first white pastor. My finely tuned, well-defined, brilliant efforts may in fact be irrelevant and possibly insulting. But my efforts are most likely good entertainment for the saints. They have been through this before and are more interested in their pastor as a person than in any particular action, program, or whatever. They consider the source as well as the action.

These assumptions alone keep me constantly reading, pondering, reflecting, and yes, planning and scheming. Despite being part time and having a busy schedule beyond the parish (I chair the local presbytery unit of eleven congregations, and my wife and I are restoring a caboose and preparing to build a house), I do have a lot of time for reading. I prefer magazines and short stories, but I am amazed by the number of books I have read during the course of a year. To be in the parish is to read. To be alone in the parish is to read a lot. To be alone in a rural parish is to read all the time. (The exaggeration is only slight.)

I live some distance from my church office. I will often spend the night in the office on a futon in order to read and work in the cool, quiet hours of the night and avoid having to drive another 104 miles round-trip. But even the drive is a good time for thought. My car knows the way by now, and the Trinity River and the coastal mountains are beautiful in every season of the year.

Not living next to the church or even just a few minutes away has both pluses and minuses. Given my nature and the present circumstances, I think the arrangement is mostly good. I need to be pulled away from my work, forced to let things go, required to be a bit more organized. The time and distance allow me to reflect upon where I have been and begin to think about where I am going before I arrive.

We assume the church can attempt to do and be a lot of things, but first and foremost it is the church. In this case, it happens to be a Presbyterian church (with some strange Lutheran touches, on Sundays in particular). As such, we may be ignored or resented for what we are, but before anything begins and after everything is said and done, we are the church. We worship, sing, pray, sin in thought, word, and deed, help the needy, celebrate Holy Communion, study the Word. We are Bible people.

I know this kind of talk makes some people wince. It has all the potential to make our congregation insensitive to the culture around and within us. But it hasn't worked out that way. We are working out our faith with fear and trembling in this time and place. One half of us are Native Americans. We must be honest about ourselves, and clear in our proclamation. If this is a stumbling block, it will be neither the first nor the last. Perhaps the issue here is integrity on both sides of the church/community line.

We assume that the church is a community, a fellowship of believers. We are here for one another. We are not perfect in anything we do or are—all the more reason we need each other. Several times a year we enjoy social gatherings and informal worship experiences with Father Ralph and our neighbors at the Blessed Kateri Tekakwitha Roman Catholic mission. We try to have at least one congregational fellowship event every month. We assume that we are here for the community. We have operated a small food closet for several years, will be reopening a thrift shop in a few months, and strongly support a community-based preschool. Funerals are held in our chapel, meetings in our community rooms, classes in our pottery shed. We are always open to new ideas that help encourage people.

One part of our church's ministry is called "This Day!" Its motto is "Organizational Support for Hoopa Valley Non-profits." Since there are few nonprofits in the valley, "This Day!" attempts to encourage the formation of grassroots groups. We have acquired a computer and a good quality copier as basic office equipment. These things are taken for granted in larger cities and churches. In missions and small towns these are often considered extras. The truth is, they are more needed here than almost anywhere else. I was pleased to learn this summer that my congregation is ahead of a congregation with twenty-five hundred members in our automation.

Remote places tend to be forgotten by churches in more populous areas. A friend of mine is a wonderful person and superb pastor. She was genuinely concerned that her congregation would not be able to continue to support us in their mission budget because we were so far away from their membership (three hundred miles). I had to point out to her that among other things "remote" means "not near anything." If they cannot reach us, there is no one who can.

Following the reunion of north and south in the Presbyterian church, administrative changes worked to the disadvantage of places like Hoopa. While the old system was complicated, it provided four formal levels of funding for Hoopa. The new system in essence says we are the responsibility of the presbytery, just one of the levels. Our presbytery has been generous and eagerly faithful in its financial and spiritual support, but it has fewer dollars to give. Our task is to attempt constantly to mend old fences and make new friends wherever we can find them.

A mission's purposes can easily become blurred. Therefore every month, and sometimes twice a month, we mail our newsletter, "COTMandoings," to over 350 individuals, congregations, and support agencies. There are many items in the newsletter, but its one message is, "Your Native American Mission Is Still Here, Alive, and Needs You."

And to be honest about it, even if no one else enjoys the newsletter, I do. The newsletter is a no-holds-barred bucket of everything from humor to local issues and events to commentary on larger church issues. People write and call asking to be added to our mailing list, although now and then we do have people who feel we are not serious enough. The computer database program allows us to sort our mailing list so that we can send postcards to local people only, to alert them to special events or to encourage a good response to some church happening.

Being rural means the pastor must travel. My cherished Volvo, "Gunnar," is five years old and has over 150,000 miles on it. Everything is a long way from wherever you happen to be. Hospital calls, committee and presbytery meetings, goodwill visits, the lot. Our budget includes one thousand dollars just for out-of-county travel, and it is not enough.

Telephone bills can be enormous, but are still less expensive than travel. We have recently joined PRESBYNET, the denominational computer network, hoping it will help keep us in touch.

All of these assumptions and factors swirl about to create a pattern that leads us to see the Church of the Mountains as a point where two cultures meet for mutual understanding and support. For example, Native Americans tend to be less concerned about future matters and more concerned about the here and now. From what I have seen in white churches concerning finances and budgets, unless you have your rocks in a row at least three years in advance, you are working at a disadvantage. It is easy to see how Native American issues often are either never really considered or are seen as "last-minute additions." Mission congregations are aware of some of the differences between the cultures and can be helpful in bridging some of the gaps.

■ III ■

Native American issues and viewpoints need to be addressed in the larger church through the system the church provides. The white culture is indeed, for better or worse, the dominant culture. As the old saying goes, "It does no good for the sheep to vote vegetarian if the wolves vote otherwise." Systems, rules, procedures, and guidelines are created to simplify administration and preserve a measure of fairness and justice by creating a level playing field for all parties. Exceptions are by definition rare or at least minimized. Other designs for structures may be as good as or better than the one adopted, but the virtue sought is consistency.

Having conceded the basic needs of a large organization, one can see that minority groups operating with different assumptions, traditions, and expectations will be at a disadvantage. Even if the larger organization could be persuaded to stop, look, and listen, it is doubtful that much could be done on a large scale, but small changes or "concessions" can and should be made. Concessions is in quotes because it may appear to a large group that the smaller group has received special treatment. In a sense it may have, but only in the sense of compensating for an organizational strength that is usually desirable but at times oppressive or insensitive. A good example of this process is affirmative action.

To understand that a just system is working against or ignoring a segment of the population of course requires some knowledge of and a working relationship with both cultures. I believe "advocacy" is the currently popular word for this ministry, although I do not think that one word says it all. Christians serve their Lord and their communities well when odd voices are heard; our cultures are enriched when the exceptions are well represented.

The Church of the Mountains also serves the church and the community when it encourages and supports work parties of youth and adults. We attempt to give each group equal measures of meaningful work around the church or in the community, educational experiences with people and places in the valley, and recreation. People who have been here and given something of themselves have a special place in their hearts for Hoopa and the tribes of this area. Every year we welcome at least five different groups.

It is important to note that we strive to have people develop a feeling for this place and its people. A one-week visit is hardly enough to even begin to understand all that is happening here and how the people live and play.

Because we are a small congregation, visiting groups with some materials and lots of volunteer labor help us maintain our buildings and grounds in good condition. Soon they will be in excellent condition. Poor, struggling congregations make a big mistake when they do not actively seek help maintaining their physical plant. The least of our fears is that people will sneer at that "fancy church." Most will see that the members care about their church. They will see we are a part of a larger family that comes, shares, and helps as needed. The family plays an important part in many cultures. It is foolish for us not to show, use, and enjoy ours.

One of the blessings the Church of the Mountains enjoys is a full, sophisticated irrigation system for our three acres. It was built and paid for by a woman who was not a formal member of the congregation but who worked wonders everywhere we look, including a tennis court. Ruth Gill led the way in rebuilding this mission with her industry, dedication, and pride in the grounds.

And my assumption is that when the time is right the Lord, the church, the congregation, or my own professional sense will tell me to pick up my stoles and books and say "Good night, Gracie!" We do what we can while we can. Things can happen to keep us at our labor for years, or to send us into the next chapters of our lives tomorrow. I believe in the Holy Spirit. In my experience, change has always been good. There have been times when I didn't think I could say that with a straight face, but now I know it is true.

Finally, I believe there is one large difference between a small mission congregation in a racial and ethnic setting and other small congregations. I sense that racial and ethnic congregations tend to be more adventuresome and courageous in their approach and style of ministry. Perhaps it is because their support tends to be fixed (but not always), or perhaps it is because they have no illusions or guilt about becoming, being, or once having been a large congregation. Or it might just be saying something about who they are, where they come from, how they understand the gospel.

At COTM we often fail. Most of what we try to do either never gets off the ground or staggers into the air only to crash and burn as another good idea "that should have worked." But we try more often than we fail. Some things do work, some things do happen. We are not discouraged. Success is not a god around here. I have been told by people who know about these things that estuaries are the nurseries of the oceans. Some might think "estuary" is just a fancy name for "backwater." But it says a lot. Some clergy may consider service in settings like Hoopa to be an unfortunate detour at best, exile at worst. Yet dramatic changes have often been spawned in remote areas of the world.

Paul tells us that God is in Christ bringing those who are "near" and those who are "afar" into a new person. I understand that to mean that no one will remain as before. We shall all experience change. It is in these small, out-of-the-way places that I believe I see the process, in part, being worked out. That it is being worked out from a different perspective in an unusual context may give us insight, maybe even wisdom.

If your career path doesn't take you through out-of-the-way places like Hoopa, Duck Valley, Hidden Gulch, or Lone Pine Crossroads, you may arrive at your goal only to discover you are lost. How would that be for irony?

■ 16 ■

The Rural Church and Evangelism

James Ayers

MORALE IS A key factor in any church's health, but in small rural churches it can take on overwhelming significance. Many people in small towns have felt the pain of decline for so long that it now seems normal. "We are the church: we nurture people's faith and make them alive in Christ, we work to bring in the kingdom of God." Most of this vision faded away long ago. Instead we feel an inevitability about the end of things. Perhaps we can hold on for a few more years, but our people are getting old and dying off. Before much longer, we'll all be gone.

People often hesitate to talk about the things that matter most to them. Since evangelism requires us to say what we believe about ultimate questions, we need high motivation and morale. With low morale, it doesn't happen.

An effective evangelism program can build morale. When we see new people coming in, hear new ideas being expressed, see new children in Sunday school, we get excited about things happening. Some may feel threatened by such changes. Overall, though, in our smaller congregations it doesn't take many new members to produce a sense that a lot of new people are joining. Morale soars. Maybe we can reach this community after all.

In most churches there are a few people who oppose out-reach. (For unknown reasons, these people sometimes end up on the evangelism committee.) Most people agree, however,

JAMES AYERS *was pastor of First Presbyterian Church in Kingman, Kansas. He is currently engaged in doctoral studies in patristics at Boston College, with an emphasis on evangelism in the early church.*

there has to be a way of reaching out with the gospel that is going to be effective without being obnoxious. They know that outreach is the right thing to do. But most churches have a hard time figuring out how to do it.

A church with caring, friendly, Christian members can do a good job in evangelism. Members may not think so, because of low morale. Yet if a small-town church can overcome the morale problem long enough to see some growth, the ongoing sense of aliveness will turn the morale around.

This process has three steps. The first involves facing the church's hesitations about its ability to evangelize. Step two deals with personal motivation. Step three looks at three examples of New Testament evangelism appropriate for smaller churches.

■ I ■

First let's look at five hesitations about small-church evangelism.

"There's no one here to evangelize." In rural communities like ours, everybody knows everybody, and we all know which families are Methodist, Baptist, Catholic, and the rest. We are convinced that there can hardly be anyone left over. In Kansas, at least, this conviction is mistaken. A recent study showed that 40 percent of the population of a typical rural Kansas community has no functional connection with any church.

This is easy to confirm in small towns where the ministerial alliance is cooperative. Four communities in our presbytery have done so. Pass around a copy of the phone book and have each church cross off the names of the people in their congregation. The phone book is thin, so it won't take long. A small number of people not crossed off may be attending church in a neighboring town, but the rest of them are not part of a church. More names will show than people expect. Sometimes only a third of the population is left unmarked, sometimes half. Even in communities that count their residents by hundreds rather than thousands, that's a sizeable number.

Because most of us interact with the same circle of friends most of the time, it's hard for us to believe there could be that many. But they are there.

"Which motivations are acceptable?" Small-church people stress outreach for one of two reasons. Either they are concerned about the church's need for new members for program and financial reasons (we need new Sunday school teachers and money for Sunday school materials), or they are concerned about individuals who are separated from God's love and purpose for them (we need to tell them the gospel so they can respond and become Christian). Opposing sides feel they know which of these concerns is right. In small churches we spend energy criticizing the motivation of those who see it the other way, because they're involved with evangelism for the "wrong reason."

But God has made different people capable of perceiving the world in different ways. Some people see the congregation, others see the individuals. If concern for our congregation moves us toward evangelism, that's good. If a sense that knowing Jesus could make a difference in the life of a particular person moves us to evangelize, that's good too. The apostle Paul thought that even when people had motives that were apparently designed to be painful to him, he could still be glad that the gospel was proclaimed (Phil. 1:15-18). We need to be just as affirming when someone has a good motivation for sharing the gospel, even though it doesn't happen to be the same thing that motivates us.

"Which program are we going to use?" Many churches invest energy debating which outreach method they should try. They never get around to using any of them. That's unfortunate, because it doesn't usually matter which program you use. Pick the one you like. If you like one and someone else likes a different one, pick both of them. You do the one that appeals to you, and let the others do the one that they feel better about.

It's like wanting to lose weight and trying to pick the diet you're going to use. There are about as many evangelism programs available in the bookstores as there are diets, and in less than an afternoon you can decide how well you like them. Pick the one that seems right to you, put it into practice, and it will work well enough.

"I might not know what to say." I have often made the mistake of misunderstanding this statement as a request for a training program, better skills, or more complete answers. Most of the time, however, the speaker really means something like the following: "It's not so much that someone might ask me a hard question. I just don't know what I ought to say if we talk about religion. Since I don't know beforehand how the conversation is likely to go, I might not know what to say."

That's true. But it's true nearly *all* the time. We don't know in advance what we're going to say about anything, but we ordinarily don't let that stop us. That would be like staying away from a party because you might not know what to say to the people sitting next to you. What if they want to talk about the weather? What if we talk about families? Or about the ball game? Or jobs? If nobody tells me beforehand how the conversation is going to go, how can I take part in it? I might not know what to say.

Since all of our conversations work that way, we ought not to expect evangelistic conversations to be any different. We will need to listen to what's going on in a person's life and see where the connections are to what's going on in our lives. Perhaps we can just talk honestly about where some of the rough spots are for us, and about how we sense God's grace enabling us to work our way through them. That kind of conversation doesn't need a script.

We don't have to have all the answers to talk about what faith in Christ means to us. What we do need is an awareness of the difference being a Christian is making. Something has to be going on inside us. We may not be able to measure it directly from one day to the next. But if we are basically at the same place in our Christian life that we were a year ago, if not much has happened that makes us aware that growth is taking place, we may have little to say. If, however, we can say, "You know, a year ago I would have reacted to these circumstances in a certain way, but now I can see how God has helped me to grow a little and enabled me to look at things differently, and by God's grace I can see that it's going to be much more helpful if I do this instead," we will have something to talk about.

"I might offend someone." The stereotypical evangelist is supposed to care only about counting the notches carved on his evangelistic gun handle. That image intimidates many of us. We fear that it will look like we're not at all interested in the persons we talk to. They'll suspect we don't care about who they are, how they feel, or what matters to them. We have seen this kind of evangelism in action. We've seen evangelistic crusades where people were emotionally manipulated until they reacted the way the leaders wanted. We've had people knock on our doors or buttonhole us in airports to convert us on the spot. We don't want to be guilty of doing the same.

Yet those who are most anxious have the least to worry about. If we don't want to be rude to people, we will make it a point to talk to them politely. If we care enough about others that we don't want to hurt their feelings, we're probably going to be careful, thoughtful, and sensitive about what we say and about how they're responding to it. If we're afraid that we're going to offend people, we're probably not going to.

■ II ■

Step two in the process of small-church evangelism involves determining our personal motivation.

In small churches we often spend time guessing what might motivate others before we figure out what motivates ourselves. We ask, "Will more people attend Sunday school—will 'they' attend—if we run a seminar on Christian families or on how to read the Bible?" It's more difficult to ask, "Will I attend those classes? Will those topics motivate me?"

Motivation begins with me. I must be willing to help people discover how faith in Christ makes a difference, starting with myself. Though we say evangelism is the right thing to do, we hesitate—not because we are unsure about how to go about it, but simply because we don't want to do it.

This reluctance can be so strong that it almost seems like people are ashamed at the idea of talking about what Jesus means to them, or what Jesus has done in their lives. My facile response has sometimes been to quote one of the great texts of the Bible. "I am not ashamed of the gospel, because it is the power of God for the salvation of everyone who believes" (Rom. 1:16). "If you are ashamed to acknowledge me before other people, I will be ashamed to acknowledge you before my Father in heaven" (Luke 9:26). When people act ashamed to tell others about their faith, I have tried suggesting that there may be more shame in not telling them.

But while some of us can be motivated—at least for a while—by a text, we need to face a deeper problem. The biblical mandate may be clear, but many people find that when they take these words seriously they just grow more miserable and ashamed. Browbeating one another with Bible verses may enable us to know what we should do (and may make us feel guilty for our failures), but it doesn't make us want to do it.

What will make us want to do it? What will motivate us to learn to do things that embarrass us? Take kissing as an example. I like kissing. There was a time in my life when I didn't, when I thought kissing was yucky. Somehow I grew out of that: at some point my attitude turned completely around, to where kissing felt like the most exciting thing in the world—right in the midst of the scariness and embarrassment. And then you had to talk about all these new feelings, about falling in love. That was scary and embarrassing, too.

I felt that way a lot, during those growing up years. I didn't want to, but it took me awhile to figure out that if I wanted to learn to kiss a girl without being embarrassed, I had to go ahead and kiss her when I was embarrassed. If I wanted to tell her about the things that mattered without being embarrassed, I had to talk about them when I was embarrassed. Because I wanted to learn how to kiss, because I wanted to be able to say, "I love you," I had to learn to keep on going in spite of the "I can't do this" feelings. I've formulated this principle as

Ayers' Law: The way you learn to do anything when you've said "I can't do it" is by doing it.

Talking with other people about your faith is like that. If you really don't want to do it, probably no one is ever going to talk you into it. But if you feel within yourself the desire to be effective in evangelism, then just go ahead and begin. Of course you won't do very well at first—no one ever does. But that is how you will learn to do it. Yes, it's scary as you first start out, and you'll make mistakes that will seem funny in the long run, though they may embarrass you at the moment.

People do respond to the open-hearted, honest sharing of their friends. They are more interested in hearing why believing in Jesus is important to us than we give them credit for. Sure, most of them don't want to be harassed. But they do want to know what makes our faith real.

■ III ■

Methods that may work in urban settings, like mass evangelism, media evangelism, and door-to-door evangelism, usually don't work well in rural settings. With a large population base, a method that alienates some people and that others ignore can still be successful. In a small town we simply don't use methods that confront and alienate people. The people here have relationships with one another that go back years or generations. They will not jeopardize these. We can't talk to people in a way that will make us embarrassed to meet them in the grocery store the next day. Yet these are often the only models that people are familiar with.

As alternatives, let's look at three New Testament evangelists in action. They suggest styles of evangelism appropriate for rural churches. They are not programs, but ministries, or gifts.

The ministry of Philip: Identification. In many of our small towns we have a feeling that we have fewer young families than we used to have. We Presbyterians surmise that they must worship with the Methodists or Baptists, because they aren't with us. When we drink coffee with our Methodist and Baptist friends, though, we discover that they don't have them either. We then take note of the fact that many of our young people leave town when they get out of school, and that our overall population is aging. There must not be as many young families as there once were, we conclude.

Well, perhaps there aren't, but the decrease is only by a small fraction. The real decline is among those in their forties and fifties, the children of the Depression and World War II, not those in their thirties, the baby boomers. In rural communities there may not be quite so many young families as there were a generation ago, but because few churches are reaching out to this age group, many of them remain unchurched. There may be more young families outside the church now than at any other time in the history of our towns—a large group of people, in fact, who may be more ready to respond to the gospel than we thought.

While many of us have a hard time believing that there could be those people out there, there are others among us who could name dozens of people who fit this description. They are individuals whom God has gifted: they can see the folks the rest of us miss, and they can recognize the people we ought to follow up on. If we can give them the freedom to engage in this kind of outreach, they will locate potential new members of the church.

But is that evangelism, or is it conducting a membership drive, as any club might? New Testament examples of people on the lookout for outsiders begin with Paul, who desired to preach Christ where he had been previously unknown (Rom. 15:20). This seems to be true also of Philip, and Philip is a less intimidating model for most of us than Paul. Philip brings Nathanael into the group of disciples—thus helping someone with a basic honesty (an Israelite indeed, in whom is "no guile") and a faith that, though hidden, is ready to be expressed ("Rabbi, you are the Son of God"), despite his cynicism ("Can anything good come out of Nazareth?"). The key to the episode is Philip, who identifies Nathanael as more ready to respond than others (including Nathanael himself) realize, and who offers the wonderfully disarming invitation, "Why don't you come and see?"

Perhaps we should recognize in this incident not merely one person talking to a friend but a particular facet of Philip's personality, a personality on the lookout for people on the outside who might be brought in. Is this why Philip is the one the Greek visitors to Jerusalem approach to find out more about Jesus (John 12:20-22)? Philip does not resolve the issue by himself. Having identified the Greeks and their needs, he apparently turns the situation over to Andrew.

If we can discover the people in our congregation who have Philip's gift and encourage them to use it, they will identify people in the community the rest of us may never have envisioned as part of the church. In rural communities there are people who have a strong faith that has never been expressed publicly. It would surprise most of the people in town to find out about it, because it is so well covered over with caution or cynicism. No one invites these people to a Sunday school class or Bible study, because we all know that they would scoff, "A church meeting? Can anything good come out of a church meeting?" Some among us have been given the ability to invite them to come and see.

The ministry of Andrew: Assimilation. Even in small churches people occasionally come to visit. Sometimes they only worship with us once, but sometimes they end up becoming active participants. How does this happen? Whether they took the first initiative to attend, or whether we invited them, something happens that advances them beyond the visitor stage.

What happens is a sense of belonging. "This is where we want to be. These are our kind of people, we feel at home here. The way they believe is the way I want to believe. The way they worship is the way I want to worship."

How do people who have been outside the body of Christ get to be part of it? How do they get into the body? It happens officially when they make a public profession of faith. But do they feel it? When do they feel that they belong, that they've been incorporated. To be "in-corporated" is to be formed into or added to the body, to be made one of the members, or one of the ingredients. The effort to assimilate or incorporate new people into the church is the effort to include them as part of the body of Christ.

Andrew is the example of the ministry of assimilation. Philip made initial contact with the Greek visitors to Jerusalem. Then Andrew took over (John 12:20-22). Andrew brought his brother Simon more firmly into the circle of the followers of Jesus (John 1:41).

The ministry of assimilation is neglected because it is difficult. Many books have been written on interpersonal evangelism, techniques, programs. But assimilation is difficult to program. How shall we visit people in the new apartment complex? We could figure out a schedule to do that. How will we incorporate the people who respond to our visits? It's hard to come up with a program for that.

There are individuals who have the gifts to make assimilation happen. Some people have been called by God to be matchmakers. They have a gift that enables them to meet people, find out about them, and know what person or group to match them up with. They say things like, "You know, someone you ought to meet is Jan. You've got a lot in common. I know she's had some of the same questions you have." Suppose the matchmaker then calls Jan and asks her to invite the newcomer out to coffee. The newcomer starts to feel at home. Jan has a new friend. The body of Christ is growing stronger with the addition of a new member. But again, the key to the whole episode is someone with this gift of matchmaking or incorporation.

Hospitality can also be part of the ministry of assimilation. Should we take more seriously the New Testament greetings offered to "So-and-so and the church that meets in their home"? It is a special gift to be able to open up one's home to people with whom a relationship has not previously been established and to help that relationship grow. There are people within our churches who would not be comfortable initiating a first-time contact with newcomers to the community, but who don't mind at all hosting a dinner for them in response to someone else's contact. Different people, different gifts.

The ministry of Barnabas: Reconciliation. One of the ongoing complaints in the rural church is that we lose people "out the back door." People once part of the church are no longer active. Did we hurt their feelings? Did they change their minds about what they believe? We don't know. All we know is that they're not here anymore, that we miss them, and we feel vaguely guilty about the whole thing.

It takes a special person to make the effort to try to reconcile these people back into the church's fellowship. It takes an ongoing effort. Sometimes our own feelings get hurt in the process, and we need to be able to keep going despite temporary discouragements.

This was the gift of Barnabas. Perhaps the most notable ministry of the "son of encouragement" is his ability to bring back or restore people. Saul might well have stayed in obscurity forever, despite his brief success in Damascus (Acts 9:22), had Barnabas not found him, first in Jerusalem (Acts 9:27), later in Tarsus (Acts 11:25-26), and brought him back to active ministry. Barnabas is able to see that Mark's failure in missionary work need not be permanent (Acts 15:36-39), and apparently his faith is justified (2 Tim. 4:11). Is it justified by the gift from God that enables him to stand by Mark and restore him to active church work?

There are people in small congregations with this gift. "I couldn't call on newcomers, but I could talk to Fred and Gladys," they say when the conversation turns to people who have drifted away from the church. They have been gifted by God with the ability to go to people the rest of us have given up on. They can often express God's grace in a way that leads people back into the circle of the church.

Some people in a rural church may feel comfortable with one of these models, but uncomfortable with the other two. I take this as evidence they have been given one spiritual gift rather than another. If people are given the freedom to exercise the particular ministry God has equipped them with, they will do it, and do it effectively. As growth then occurs, and as we allow ourselves to see it, a gradual shift in morale can start to take place. As the morale (slowly) begins to improve, as the sense of "We're not a dying church, we're a living and growing church" increases, the motivation increases as well—motivation to try new things, to keep on going, to exercise the particular gifts that God has given to us as individuals, and to reach out to new people and see them become members of the body of Christ.

■ *17* ■

A Place Called Home

Susan M. Fleenor

MY BEGINNINGS found me cradled in a small country church in rural Idaho. It was from my mother's knee and my father's arms that I slowly moved down the wooden pew to make room for my four sisters and two brothers. It was many a Sunday morning, within the aisles of those pine pews, that I was introduced to Moses, King David, Esther, Isaiah, Ruth, God the Creator, Jesus of Nazareth, Mary Magdalene, and others. It was memory verses like "For God so loved the world," hymns like "Blessed Assurance," and prayers like "Thine is the kingdom, and the power, and the glory, forever," that were sown and nurtured in my being. It was Christmas carols piercing the cold winter nights and the silent meditations of Easter morning dawns that echoed my beginnings in a Christian community.

Many memories are blurred now, but the ones that are most vivid center on the experience of the church as family and extended family. When I recall these memories and picture myself in that time and in that place, love and devotion for that small country church and its people well up. It was there, in the life and ministry of that church, that I felt most at home. It was home—a relaxed, comfortable, familiar, and intimate place where I was loved.

The memory that I often call upon and that is characteristic of my experience of the small church as a place called "home" began on a typical Sunday morning. The same folks—about forty in all, names and faces all familiar to me—settled into their pews as they did every Sunday morning. Mrs. Roberts, my second-grade teacher; Cornie, Donna, Greg, and Eileen

SUSAN M. FLEENOR *is pastor of Heritage Presbyterian Church in Benicia, California.*

Lanting, close friends of the family; Mildred Jones, an elder; Uncle Ben and Aunt Evelyn, to name a few, all gathered for fellowship and the worship of God. My cousin Melva and I sat in the front pew by ourselves that morning, in full view of Reverend Thomas, and perhaps that made all the difference. Halfway through the service he stepped out from the pulpit. Through spectacles he focused his aged yet sensitive eyes in our direction and invited all those who wished to make a public declaration of faith in Jesus Christ and follow in Christ's way to step forward and stand with him. My cousin, older than me by ten days, did not hesitate. At her response, not wanting to be left behind, I bolted from the pew to stand with her. A few Sundays later, my cousin seemingly forgotten though I'm sure she was present, the memory is of my grandfather, who stepped forward that day following my earlier initiative. Feeling quite uncomfortable in his occasional Sunday suit, he nervously knelt to be touched with the water of baptism and was welcomed into the body of Christ. Standing proudly beside him was a twelve-year-old girl who professed her trust in Jesus Christ as Lord and Savior as well. I was that young girl. I don't necessarily remember my confession of faith, but I do remember my grandfather and the depth and breadth of his "I do!" shaped by seventy-plus years of toil and laughter. My Grandpa Fleenor died a few years later.

I cannot fully explain why this experience is so significant to me. I suppose it could be called my conversion experience, and certainly a confirmation that I belonged to the household of God. The church of Jesus Christ was my home, and I felt most at home, most at ease, in a congenial and familiar environment that can best be described as small church. Understanding myself to that degree has certainly shaped my vocation in the church and my style of ministry as a small church pastor.

■ I ■

Shortly after becoming pastor of the church I now serve, a young woman began worshiping regularly with her husband and two small children. At one Sunday worship during the sharing of joys and concerns, she rose to her feet and expressed her and her family's joy at being a part of this fellowship. She went on to say with a touch of emotion, "I feel like I've come home." I could identify with her feelings, and it wasn't the first time, nor would it be the last, that I had heard people express similar thoughts. On the other hand, I have seen many pass through the church, never settling down, never sensing that this particular church was the place for them to become personally attached. One can't help asking, "What is at the heart of those who feel at home in a particular church?"

Several things come to mind. A sense of being on familiar ground, which helps a person feel at ease and in harmony with those who also call the church their home. A sense of being known by others, not only by name, but at a more significant level. A sense of being cared about and valued. A sense of being needed, of finding a place to serve and make a vital contribution to this church's life and ministry. A sense of being connected, bound to others by the ties of family and friendship. And a sense of ownership, being able to claim and affirm the church as "my" church. If there is one word that can sum this all up, I believe that word is "belonging." It's a matter of understanding that this is where I fit in, where I am included, where I am one of the family, and where I've chosen even if unconsciously to give my allegiance and loyalty.

As people's lives change, though, they may begin to wonder and perhaps doubt whether they really belong. The adolescent years that followed my confession of faith were uneventful for the most part. Before long I left the security of my family and my church community and ventured into college and then into marriage. One Saturday morning three years into that marriage, the man I loved and hoped would be my life partner forever presented me with divorce papers. I was overwhelmed with a rush of emotions that did not fully subside for years. My heart and my spirit were in critical condition. I felt as if I had been cast into the wilderness and was in danger of being lost there. What was I to do? Somehow I knew that all I could do was return home. Once I was home my parents graciously insisted that I join them for worship. I was reluctant. I was aching and scared. Would the church of my childhood accept me? Would they bear with me in this darkness of my soul?

I discovered that this small country church had not changed much in seven years. Although sisters, cousins, and grandparents were no longer a part of the congregation, I was not among strangers. They knew me. They cared for me. And unknowingly perhaps they provided me with a safe place to recover from my wounds and wrestle with my God. Taking refuge in their loving embrace was the beginning of healing. To claim the church as home, one must be able to experience the unconditional love one needs at times from the Christian family. To be at home is to be in a place and in a community where folks are committed to you and you to them no matter what. This happened for me in this small church.

As the pain subsided and life seemed a possibility for me again, I became more aware of the leading of God's Spirit. Every Sunday in the summer of my twenty-seventh year, I stood in the pulpit of my home church and sought to preach the good news of Jesus Christ. It seemed somewhat ironic that the hearers of the Word were the very people who had been the Word, the instruments of God's good news to me. But perhaps it was ironic to them as well, that the child of five they remembered with braided hair and skinned knees was now an adult, ready to leave the nest a second time and take full flight. As we worshiped together that summer, I came to understand that God was calling me to the ministry of Word and Sacrament. With their prayers and blessings, I was sent off to seminary. Once again I chose to leave the security of a familiar and intimate place. This time I left wondering whether I would ever "belong" as I had belonged in that small church.

■ **II** ■

Three years later, on the verge of graduation from seminary and in pursuit of a pastoral call, the question took a slightly different turn: Where would God have me belong as a pastor, what particular church would I be calling "home"? Many seminary-related folks were encouraging me to seek a staff position. For me that implied a larger church than I was accustomed to. I could have followed their counsel, but I would not have been faithful to my experience, gifts, or identity. The small church was all I knew, and I couldn't imagine being anything but a small church pastor. I received a call to a church in rural Idaho, just thirty-five miles from my home church. I did not accept the call, but it made me struggle with whether it was my duty and obligation to return to the home folks of southern Idaho. Seminary, however, had changed my theological perspective somewhat, living in Berkeley had broadened my worldview, a new extended family of friends bound my heart to northern California. God's Spirit had other plans. I would not be going home, but I would be heading homeward to a place of God's choosing.

One Saturday afternoon, friends and I decided to drive to Lake Berryessa for a picnic. Knowing that the following week I would be interviewing with the pastor-seeking committee from the Pioneer Presbyterian Church of Winters, we took a few moments to tour this rural agricultural town, the "Gateway to the Monticello Dam." Without too much difficulty we located the church, actually a social hall where worship was held. The doors were locked. No one was around, but I took the liberty to walk around the building and peer through the windows. I returned to the car. My friends tell me I was aglow with joy. Intuitively I knew that Winters was to be my new home. To the surprise of the presbytery, who assumed this church would never call a woman, I was called, to my delight and thanks. Later, members of the committee lovingly said that I had "wooed" them.

"Pioneer" was an appropriate name for this small church and my first pastorate. It was founded in 1875. Vernie Johnston, grandson of the founding pastor, was still worshiping faithfully at the age of ninety. At least 40 percent of the congregation was made up of retired folks and widows. I was ministering mostly to and with people my parents' and grandparents' ages.

Unlike some of my colleagues in ministry who are called to communities and parishes that are foreign to their experiences, I was fortunate in that I did not have to recover from culture shock, but could easily settle in with these easygoing, home-grown farm and country folk like myself. But I wasn't called there to work the land or harvest the apricots, I was there to provide pastoral care and spark new growth. Once again, though, I began to struggle with the question of belonging, for how could a "thirty-something" baby boomer like myself minister to the needs of people much longer-lived than me?

I discovered that I did indeed belong, not so much because of what I did (other than to get to know them by name and learn their stories), but because of how I was cared for and nurtured by this aging congregation. In terms of the pastoral role and its responsibilities, I often felt like a child—a toddler really—learning how to walk, but often resorting to crawling. I was just a babe in ministry, and I had much to learn. But persons like Glenn Kidder, a gentle, loving gem of a man, much like my father, was there to encourage me with his smile, his touch, his humor. Persons like Genevie Dexter, fondly known by many as a "little banny chicken," were there to spark my desire to keep on keeping on with her own enthusiastic, generous, empowering spirit, much like my mother's. Cared for by people that I could have easily called "dad" or "mom" or "grandma," I was at home.

The assurance that I was truly a part of them came, I believe, when I readily shared in and helped fulfill their dream. Their dream for decades had been to build a new sanctuary on the very spot where the original building had sat prior to being torn down in the 1950s. Such a dream and its fulfillment gave witness to this small church's commitment to provide a place for the generations that would follow, a place where children, youth, and adults would find Christian fellowship and inspiration for joyful, compassionate Christian living and service.

■ III ■

Once the dream was realized and the complexion of the congregation gradually began to change with the addition of children and young families, I became restless. It was as if I had accomplished what God had intended for me in this community of faith. As a single woman, serving the only mainline Protestant denomination in town, I felt isolated and far removed from the network of support established in seminary. But how could I possibly leave? How could I abandon my Pioneer family? As I struggled with that question and pondered how difficult it was for a woman to receive a second call, I simply waited on God in prayer.

As I neared my fifth anniversary as pastor of Pioneer Church, I quite accidently learned that a small church in Benicia was seeking a pastor. Their committee was nearing the end of their search process, and, spurred by the Spirit, I forwarded to them my dossier with a cover letter, asking them to consider me. And I asked myself, "Could God possibly call me, a simple farm girl, to a new-church-development church in suburbia?"

Today I am entering my third year as pastor of Heritage Church in Benicia. On World Communion Sunday, the church will celebrate the seventh anniversary of its charter. Though its history is short, 60 percent of the charter members have already left in response to a crisis. I am in a redevelopment of a new church development. The soul of the church is those who chose to remain, committed to Christ and his church, believing God wanted a Christian fellowship like Heritage in Benicia, no matter what. They are a people with a vibrant and joyful spirit that is contagious.

At the present time I find myself ministering with and to a congregation that is primarily of my own generation, some with children now entering college and others just starting their families. I feel at times as if I am back in the household of my birth, living and playing with siblings. But instead of being the oldest child, without an elder brother or sister to pave the way into adolescence and adulthood, I am in partnership with contemporaries, and with those in this Christian fellowship who were journeying with God long before I learned my first memory verse. Encouraged and inspired by their witness, I am striving to be faithful to the trust they have placed in me as their pastor.

Sometimes, though, I wonder whether I really belong. On occasion I am homesick for Winters. I miss the sight of almond and cherry orchards in bloom, and sitting with "Pop" cracking walnuts. I miss not knowing and being known by the mayor and his family and being with friends who own and edit the local newspaper. But I trust that this is a place of God's own choosing and thus my home for now.

The struggle with belonging most often arises when others share their pain and question whether they are really counted among this church's family. Not long ago a woman recounted to me how difficult it was at times to be a part of this fellowship as a single woman. Recently while sharing coffee and conversation with folks following worship, this woman felt painfully excluded. A couple that she had reached out to in a time of illness invited the family she was visiting with to dinner that evening. She longed to be included, but instead was wounded by the sting of rejection. I am sure the hostess-to-be was unaware of the pain she had inflicted. Even the small church is not always an inviting, hospitable place for people because of their marital status, social background, economic situation, age, political leanings, physical capabilities, or sexual orientation.

It seems, then, that part of my calling to Heritage is as much a call to make of this church a home not only for myself and its membership but for all who are looking for a welcoming place to put down roots even for a short time, the kind of roots that will bring forth fruit in the service of God and neighbor.

The roots of some were nurtured and strengthened recently as I invited and encouraged nine families to make a commitment to an educational, intergenerational, and celebrative experience called "Family Cluster." Every Sunday evening for eight weeks, after we had shared a potluck meal, all twenty-eight of us would gather in a circle on the sanctuary floor. In that circle we shared treasures and stories, we hugged and we prayed, we sang and we danced, we laughed, and more, all the while affirming and experiencing the church as family and extended family. And in those precious moments we were at home in each other's presence. I believe that was as true for one-year-old Nathaniel, whose joy was wonderfully infectious, as it was for Jona, widow and grandmother, whose gentle spirit soothed us all. As for me, I, too, was one of the family. The experience was reminiscent of my beginnings in the church, but now I was also the pastor, called to direct our attention to God, "from whom every family in heaven and on earth is named" (Eph. 3:15).

Each Family Cluster evening was brought to an end with the singing of Bob Gillman's song "Bind Us Together."

> Bind us together, Lord, bind us together
> with cords that cannot be broken.
> Bind us together, Lord, bind us together,
> bind us together with love.
>
> There is only one God. There is only one King.
> There is only one body, that is why I sing.
>
> Bind us together, Lord, bind us together
> with cords that cannot be broken.
> Bind us together, Lord, bind us together,
> bind us together with love.*

With such singing, I could not help recalling and celebrating the moment my heart was truly bound to God and to the body of Christ. It was the very moment that my parents presented me for baptism and the minister said to them, "God our Father, who has redeemed us by the sacrifice of Christ, is also the God and Father of our children. They belong, with us who believe, to the membership of the church through the covenant made in Christ, and confirmed to us by God in this sacrament, which is a sign and seal of our cleansing, of our engrafting into Christ, and of our welcome in the household of God." With my parents' affirmation of faith and the sprinkling of some water, I was received into Christ's Church. I belonged. To this day I understand baptism primarily as a sacrament of belonging, in which we are accepted into the ministry and mission of the church in response to and for the glory of God. So now with

---

*Maranatha! Music Praise Chorus Book, Costa Mesa, California: Maranatha! Music, 1983, p. 63.

each baptism I witness and of which I am a part, I promise with God's help to welcome God's own with open arms, and to create for them a familiar and intimate place called home. To all those who made and continue to make it so for me I am indeed grateful.

■ 18 ■

Prepared after All

Douglas J. Hale

IT WAS HOLY SATURDAY. I was preparing to leave my apartment and climb the hill to the Easter vigil. The phone rang. It was an expected call. For much of what was said I was prepared. For the practical results of the call, however, I was both prepared and unprepared.

A district superintendent of my United Methodist conference was calling to tell me about my first pastoral appointment. I knew the chances were good it would be a small church far from the beaten track. What I was unprepared for was how far off the beaten track a person can get. I discovered later that I was going to be two hours from the nearest church of my own denomination, at the extreme north edge of my conference, over four thousand feet in the air.

That was in Idaho. The next year I was appointed to two rural and small-town churches in Oregon. The image I had in my mind of the churches I would serve was of a small suburban church or a church in a small town near an urban center. My image of a pastor was one of a professional. No one had told me the image of a missionary was more appropriate. On reflection, I realized the missionary was far more common in my denomination's history, with its circuit riders and rural evangelists, than the professional.

At seminary the big issues were divestment of South African stocks, full inclusion of homosexuals into the church and society as a whole, full inclusion of women in language and practice, and work for economic justice in Third World countries, especially in Central America.

DOUGLAS J. HALE *is pastor of the United Methodist Churches in Sutherlin and Wilbur, Oregon.*

181

When I left seminary, I discovered that the big issues in the rural communities where I was headed were quite different. Economic issues focus on the deterioration of the lumber, mining, and farming industries. Who in these communities has money to invest in South Africa? Another issue is the effect of tourism on the jobs available and where the tourism money eventually ends up. Teenage pregnancy is an issue. Skyrocketing taxes are becoming destructive. There is a growing sense in the community that people's lives, work, and church are increasingly controlled by people outside the community, in urban centers. All these are what most concern the people I was about to meet.

■ I ■

When I arrived in Idaho, one of the common subjects of conversation was the number of high school girls getting pregnant. Many adults were distressed about the bad example this presented to other girls in the school, where all ages were contained in the same building. Particular concern was expressed regarding the college-bound girls who became pregnant during their senior year and either never left town or returned after their first semester in college to have their babies and settle into being mothers and wives.

A citizens' committee on sex education formed and eventually gained the support of the school board and superintendent. I was asked to participate. After taking part for some time, I became dissatisfied with what we were trying to do. It seemed too shallow. I suspected a deeper root to this problem. Teenage pregnancy was just a symptom. I speculated that the girls were getting pregnant as a way of gaining control in their lives, of having something they could call their own, of having a purpose in a town where there were not many job or career options for women. Motherhood is wonderful. For teenage girls, however, it often meant staying where it was safe instead of venturing out into a big, threatening world.

And why were the boys being irresponsible? Were they being stupid, selfish, or sinister, preying on females for the sport of it? Again I suspected there was a deeper reason. Seminary, however, had not given me an interpretive or analytical framework that would allow me to go deeper.

What our committee did know was that a town forty miles away had a sex education program that seemed to have eliminated their teenage pregnancy problems. They were using materials called *Choices* (for girls) and *Challenges* (for boys). The program addressed not only the physical aspects of sex but also relationships, self-esteem, and life and career goal setting.

Then in October 1986, *Psychology Today* came out with two articles dealing with teenage pregnancy and sex education. One article reviewed research showing that teenagers can become pregnant out of "hopelessness, the feeling that opportunities in life are few and limited and one might as well have a baby as do anything else." There are also indications that teenagers desire spontaneous, unprotected sex because it is more forgivable if you are "swept off your feet" or under the influence of alcohol than if sex is premeditated. It seems to be preferable to plead "temporary insanity" than to have control over your life.

■ **II** ■

My first impression of our town in Idaho was that it was isolated. It wasn't near an interstate. It was two hours from the nearest city. I imagined what a missionary must feel heading out to a new mission field. The picture of a small, self-sufficient town filled my thoughts.

Soon after arriving, I began to realize that the town was not so isolated or self-sufficient as it may once have been. It used to take days to travel to the city, instead of two hours. Cars have improved. The highway is good in most places. People are used to taking a whole day—once a week sometimes—to do major shopping in the city, where they also go for jury duty.

There is also TV. Several statewide channels and cable are available, and satellite dishes have popped up in many yards. Homes are not even isolated on the inside. They have been invaded by the media bringing them news, sports, drama, and the rest from every place but that little town. You can be in Boise, Portland, Atlanta, Chicago, and around the world with the push of a button or the turn of a dial.

This town, which at one time had most of the basic services that a town needs, now has little of its own commerce. Even the grocery store is little more than an oversized convenience store. To do real shopping, you have to go to the town twelve miles away. That is where most of the businesses have gone. Or perhaps it should be said, the businesses in that town have replaced the ones in the smaller town that have died out. Along the main road where businesses used to be are vacant store-fronts, empty lots, and the remains of fire-gutted shells whose debris has been removed.

Of course the town-drain does not stop there. The distant city provides many services at cheaper prices. State government is there, and it controls many of the concerns of the town. Then there is Washington, D.C., the center of control of the federal land that completely surrounds the community. Tendrils from everywhere seem to be wrapping around the lives of the people. Is this town isolated?

When I moved to Oregon, the situation was different but the dynamics much the same. This town was going through a governmental crisis. The voters refused to pass an operating levy, so the city council shut down the police department and laid off the paid firefighters. The people had revolted. They refused to pay any more taxes. The frustration I have heard voiced is directed not just at the city. It has to do with the citizens' lack of control over taxes and how the money is spent. The state is looking for a better way to finance the schools. The solution will undoubtedly be further centralization of the taxing system, both receipts and disbursals. As the people saw control of their lives moving to the state capital and elsewhere, they struck back at the one place over which they still felt they had control—their own town.

The construction of the interstate through the town was a major event. Much land had to be reshaped to accommodate this strip of asphalt. Dynamite was used, and deep slices were gouged out of the hills. As a result of the construction of this easier way to get from city to city, many of the town's wells, which had served people so faithfully, dried up. The water tables had been disturbed by the construction, so people could no longer get water from their own land. Many had to tie into the neighboring city's water supply. This is a parable of what has happened to this town. The progress of cities has resulted in the drying up of the resources of the town. Now the town is dependent on the city for resources it once provided for itself.

Like the Idaho town, this town has vacant storefronts and empty lots. It is a victim of what has been termed the "sixty-mile city." An urban center twelve miles down the interstate and a much larger city sixty miles down the interstate have drained much of this town's economic life. It is still a victim of the recession that greatly decreased the vitality of the lumber industry in the area. Property values have decreased. Lots have gone vacant. Tax rates have had to rise simply in order to maintain services. Many of the citizens are now frantically looking for solutions to this crisis, but with little creativity.

■ III ■

The issue of control became clearer to me one day during a work weekend at a small United Methodist camp close to my church in Idaho. People from several different churches came to this camp. Some had worked for the good of the camp for decades.

A number of us were gathered in the kitchen cleaning up dishes. We were using a new three-hole sink acquired from another camp to bring this camp up to health department specifications. In the process of installation, it was discovered the sink did not meet the specifications. Some people became quite frustrated. Finally one of the old-time supporters said, "Of course, we have to do what *Portland* says!" his voice filled with anger and cynicism. With that word, "Portland," I realized that he had said it all.

Portland is where the office of our Annual Conference is located. It houses the bishop's office, and the offices of the council director and associate director. The Portland area is where most of the churches in the Annual Conference are situated. When many of the Annual Conference boards meet, they meet in Portland. Whether accurately or not, Portland symbolizes the power that controlled the efforts of the local people. Clergy are assigned from Portland. The amounts set for missions and denominational expenses come from there. Portland controls local church property development. Nothing was to be done to develop the camp without permission from "Portland."

This old man did not have the patience he once had to put up with the red tape that controlled the operation and development of the camp. At the same time, the younger ones on the site committee had developed the attitude that it was easier to ask for forgiveness than permission. Consequently, that year, with local money and volunteer labor, a bunkhouse was built without the required permission from the appropriate Annual Conference board. What would the board do, come and tear down the bunkhouse?

Now there was new energy for the camp. Unlike previous years, when the work weekend had brought out just the handful of longtime supporters, this year there were over twenty people present. The people had begun to find ways to take some control of their own camp, even if those ways were still minor in comparison with what they wanted to do.

■ **IV** ■

Outside control is not a new problem. In *The Tribes of Yahweh*, Norman Gottwald identifies such forces at work within Israel's tribal period. Later these same dynamics occurred in the time of Solomon in Judah and Omri and Ahab in Israel. It is this later period that is represented by 2 Kings 2:23-25, the story of the prophet Elisha being mocked by boys of the city of Jericho. Elisha curses them, and they are subsequently attacked by two bears. Whatever else we might think of this story, it reflects a rural-urban antagonism. Elisha was a protector of the interests of rural people as they collided with urban interests. The story is about the vindication of their hero's power in the face of the taunts of those from the city that claimed he was powerless by calling him "bald one."

People look for heroes who will make up for their relative powerlessness. In Jesus' day, those claiming to be the messiah sought to lead the people in rebellion against those who were in control. When Peter identified Jesus as the messiah, the people's protector who would set them free from those who controlled their lives, Jesus readily accepted the designation. But in the face of Peter's assumption that Jesus would free them through an uprising, Jesus had to redefine the role of the messiah. The way of the messiah was the way of being willing to give up one's life for others, rather than the way of taking the lives of the enemy (Mark 8:27-38). The focus of Jesus' ministry was on the people who were suffering, not on those who were causing the suffering.

People often look for Elishas to fight for them. People often look to their pastors to be their hero, and pastors often want to be the people's hero. But even Elisha was more of a healer and empowerer than a fighter. The stories of direct confrontation with those in control are exceptional in the accounts of the ministries of Elisha and Jesus. Most of their time was spent empowering those who felt hopeless.

■ **V** ■

One day while in Idaho, I decided to visit a young woman who had begun to get involved in the church. As I approached her small house, out in the middle of the pasture, I expected to stay for about an hour. I ended up spending four and a half hours and having dinner with her family. The conversation had begun like so many others, with small talk and discussion of where she had lived and what her interest in the church was. But then the conversation became significant in a different way. We began to talk about the town.

We both recognized the depressed atmosphere that dominated the community. The people had little hope that things would get better in their community, for they saw little chance of things going back to the way they were before. But this woman saw a sign of hope in the business venture of two brothers who reopened a gas station and began to develop it to specialize in serving the many trucks coming through town. They took advantage of the strategic location of the town, at the point where the two north-south highways meet. She saw that these two men were able to do what many other people in town were afraid to do, to take a chance and change the way things are done.

In her Iowa Humanities Lecture "Small Town: A Close Second Look at a Very Good Place," author Carol Bly has described this risk-taking as true leadership, a quality often apparently lacking in small towns. Yet she sees this as a quality that resides in all of us, and people can be shown how to make it a part of who they are. People's imaginations need to be awakened so that they can once again consider new possibilities for their present situation.

Bly focuses on how we converse with one another. All too often, people's new ideas are met not with wonder but with summarizing and discounting that belittles the idea. Or with small talk. Or with discussion of sensational events picked up through the media that have little to do with people's lives and squeeze out significant discussions about their lives. Bly's solution is to develop "interactionary" skills. When people share ideas, they need to be met with questions that seek more information about the subject and about how the person feels about it. At the same time, the listeners need to be developing mental pictures of what is being described.

Such an approach can help people clarify the sources of their frustration and anger over their present situation. Too often people place their anger inaccurately, as people in this Oregon town directed their anger at the city government. When the people shut down the police and paid fire department, they did not help their situation. They have lashed out at a handy target, but they have not effectively dealt with their frustrations over taxation and lack of representation in government. Previously they had sought to fill the city council with new members and hire a new city manager. They wanted heroes to come and solve their problems, but they have not been satisfied. They need to be encouraged to ask questions in such a way that they are able to identify the true source of their frustration and so begin to find a constructive means of resolution for their problems.

■ VI ■

During my first summer at seminary, I lived next door to Mortimer Arias. I had run head-on into Latin American liberation theologies and it seemed to me there was no one better than he, an exiled Bolivian Methodist bishop and a liberation theologian in his own right, to whom I could express my discomfort and my hopes for helpful dialogue.

After listening to my concerns, he told me that we North Americans must quit borrowing Latin American liberation theologies and create our own. This makes sense, considering that much of the genius of liberation theologies is that they are contextualized. Much time was spent in seminary focusing on Third World issues. These are important. For North Americans, however, they cannot substitute for the application of the gospel to our own context. Much energy was expended on describing the plight of peasant farmers, but not on the epidemic foreclosures on family farms and the high rates of unemployment in timber regions in the United States. A Center for Responsible Tourism took up residence at the seminary to address the impact of North Americans traveling in Third World countries. It was not clear, however, that at the same time it would speak to the impact of a town's increased dependence upon tourist dollars in the United States.

■ VII ■

I began by saying that I was in part unprepared for the ministry I found myself called to after seminary. I may have been more prepared if I had been preparing myself to be a missionary rather than a professional. I don't mean a missionary in the sense of a paternal figure going to help the helpless. I think of it more in the sense of going some place to do ministry that presents challenges and issues that are different from those experienced up to that time. I assume that people in the local situation have a great deal more information about their circumstances than I, and that what I have to bring to them is a probing and nudging that will help them identify their true problems and discover their own ways of addressing their problems.

Ministry in this form is the act of empowerment. It is ministry that seeks to liberate people from ways of thinking about their situations that keep them from taking constructive steps in solving their own problems. It is bringing a message to people that God has created them with a great deal more potential for creativity than they tend to recognize in themselves. It is a message that proclaims that the resources are not just found in the cities, even if cities do try to suck the life out of the surrounding countryside. The life of God is found within each place and each individual. It is a message that liberates.

Maybe I was not so unprepared after all.

For Further Reading

Carroll, Jackson W. *Small Churches Are Beautiful*. San Francisco: Harper & Row, 1977. Small churches have unique opportunities, illustrated here in ten essays by different authors on images of the small church, shared ministry, resources, programming, organization, and other topics.

The Christian Ministry 19, 5 (September–October 1988). Issue featuring the small church, with articles on the special strengths of the small church, inner-city ministry in a small church, preaching in relation to the agricultural crisis, and involving all members in the ministry of the church.

Dudley, Carl S., and Douglas Alan Walrath. *Developing Your Small Church's Potential*. Valley Forge: Judson Press, 1988. Two experienced interpreters combine forces in a stimulating analysis. Watch for further publications in this publisher's new Small Church in Action series.

Hassinger, Edward W., John S. Holik, and J. Kenneth Benson. *The Rural Church: Learning from Three Decades of Change*. Nashville: Abingdon Press, 1988. A detailed but brief and highly readable report on a thirty-year study of ninety-nine rural churches based on surveys in 1952, 1967, and 1982, by three rural sociologists. Extremely informative.

Hopewell, James F. *Congregation: Stories and Structures*. Philadelphia: Fortress, 1987. About all congregations, but based on a study of two churches in a small town. Shows how congregations can be understood by approaching them as an ethnographer might approach another society, seeking to discover the narrative and drama at the core of its identity. Incorporates insights from hermeneutics and literary criticism.

Schaller, Lyle E. *Looking in the Mirror: Self-Appraisal in the Local Church*. Nashville: Abingdon Press, 1984. An incisive guide to enhanced congregational self-understanding.

———— *The Small Church Is Different*. Nashville: Abingdon Press, 1982. An analysis of methods and techniques of small church ministry set against the typical expectations of large church ministry. Topics of particular interest include congregational self-esteem, youth ministry, finances, church growth, staffing, and Sunday school. The dynamics of small church congregations are carefully analyzed.

Surrey, Peter J. *The Small Town Church.* Nashville: Abingdon Press, 1981. A fictional exchange of sage and entertaining letters illustrates the approaches, trials, and triumphs of small church ministry.

Walrath, Douglas Alan, ed. *New Possibilities for Small Churches.* New York: The Pilgrim Press, 1983. A collection of essays by different authors on worship, pastoring, ethnic/minority pastors, women pastors, judicatory interventions, and small church power, edited by a church-planning consultant, who wrote a fascinating first chapter.

Warner, R. Stephen. *New Wine in Old Wineskins: Evangelicals and Liberals in a Small-Town Church.* Berkeley: University of California Press, 1988. A history of a small-town church in California from 1959 to 1982 by a sociologist. It shows how both evangelical and liberal pastors with radical religious aspirations attempted to change a small-town church, and how the church responded to their efforts.

Willimon, William H., and Robert L. Wilson. *Preaching and Worship in the Small Church.* Nashville: Abingdon Press, 1980. Members of small churches typically come together to be together. This book focuses on ways the minister can respond to this special character of the small congregation through preaching, the sacraments, and services like weddings and funerals.